Drink Yourself Thin

100
Healthy
Smoothie
Recipes

Kirk Castle

Healthy Smoothie Recipes

With More Than 100+ Healthy Delicious Smoothie Recipes That are Quick, Easy To Make and Taste Great. Your Healthy Journey Starts Here!

By Kirk Castle

Firstly, I would like to thank you for taking the opportunity to purchase my book. You've made a great decision and a step in the right direction towards healthy living. Please also take this opportunity to write a review on Amazon and help me improve this book for future editions.

Visit my other titles!

http://www.amazon.com/dp/B00A285HEY

http://www.amazon.com/dp/B00A69TTUC

http://www.amazon.com/dp/B00AMU1YJ4

© 2012 Kirk Castle

Disclaimer

This book serves as a guide for healthy living and aims to help you incorporate more green leafy vegetables, raw fruit and natural foods in your daily diet. It doesn't claim or guarantees a cure to any disease, sickness or ailments.

What we choose to put into our bodies will ultimately determine our health. That being said, it's important to have a balanced diet with all the nutritional requirements the body needs which you simply can't get from one smoothie.

It's always a good idea to consult a health professional or nutritionist before making any drastic change to your diet but adding smoothies to your daily food intake can only prove to be more beneficial than damaging.

Table of Contents

Introduction 8

The Benefits of Healthy Smoothies 12

Let's Get Started! 17

Buying & Storing Tips 20

How to Grow Your Own Greens 26

Sample Diet Plans 32

How to Make Your Smoothies 41

Recipes 64

   Healthy Smoothie Template Recipe 64

   Little-or-No-Fruit Healthy Smoothie 67

   Aloe and Apple 69

   Arugula Arame Attack 70

   Asian Healthy smoothie 70

   Beet Blast 71

   Big Black Cabbage Cocktail 72

   Black Kale Blackberry Brew 73

   Blended Salad 74

   Broccoli Blitz 74

   Brussels Blaster 75

   Butterhead Brew 76

   Cabbage Cool-Aid 77

   Carrot Top Concoction 78

Chia Choice 79

Cranapple Yogurt Crave 80

Dandelion Delight 81

Dilly Summer Drink 81

Endive Energy Express 82

Everything + The Kitchen Sink Garden Smoothie 83

Glorious Green Leaf 83

Gobs of Goji 84

Grapefruit Cilantro Booster 85

Green Chocolate Cooler 86

Kale Tangelo Tonic 87

Key Lime Broccosprout Blend 87

Kiwi Banana Krush 88

The Kumquat Question 89

Late-Summer Apricot Watercress Divine 89

Latin Healthy smoothie 90

Mango Meltaway 91

Melon-Seed Melange 91

Mixed Green Maca Madness 92

Mustard Greens Mambo 93

One Really Grape Smoothie 93

Pear Date Puree 94

Pollen Persimmon Potpourri 95

Pomegranate Potion 96

Rad Raspberry Radicchio 97

Red Leaf Rocks 97

Red Pepper Mint Julep 98

Red Smoothie 99

Romaine Rounder 99

Savory Sweet-Hot Smoothie 100

Smooth Sunflowers 101

Sodium Dandelion Blast 101

South Pacific Healthy smoothie..102

Southern Turnip-Collard Watermelon Cooler...103

Sweet Beet Slam...104

Tomato Tonic..104

Watercress Avocado Dream 105

Peach-Mango Green Smoothie...106

"Post Workout" Smoothie..106

Glow Inside and Out Ultimate Green Smoothie...107

Easy Kid-Friendly Green Smoothie...108

Green Java...109

Chocolate Green Smoothie...109

Green Jungle Monkey Smoothie...110

Cheerful Cherry Green Smoothie..111

Tropical Pineapple..111

Kale and Banana Smoothie...112

Berry Smoothie with Bee Pollen...112

Kale and Pear Smoothie..113

Banana-Orange Green Smoothie...114

Green Protein Smoothie..114

Healthy Green Coconut Smoothie...115

Ginger-Carrot with Pineapple Smoothie...115

Apple-Pineapple Tropical Fusion Green Smoothie 116

Tropical Pineapple-Papaya Green Smoothie..117

Meal Replacement Green Smoothie..117

Cherry-Citrus with Dandelion Greens Smoothie..118

Raw Food Breakfast Smoothie..119

"The Newbie" Smoothie..120

Organic Green Smoothie...120

Alcohol Detox Smoothie...121

Strawberry-Raspberry Heart Healthy Smoothie..122

Green Drink...122

Heart Healthy Smoothie...123

6

The Healthy Green 124

Groovy Green Smoothie 125

Cashew Peach Green Smoothie 125

Blueberry Green Smoothie with Almond Butter 126

Green Smoothie with Peanut Butter 126

Blueberry Green Smoothie 127

Banana Mango Green Smoothie 128

Summer Blueberry Green Smoothie 128

Mango Banana Green Smoothie 129

High Protein Green Smoothie 130

Cleansing Green Smoothie with Parsley 130

Kickin' Kale Strawberry Smoothie 131

Kale Smoothie with Pear 132

Kale Smoothie with Papaya 132

Green Lightening 133

Mango Green 134

Berry Blast 134

Velvety Green Smoothie 135

Delightful Strawberry 135

Zesty Banana 136

Cool Mint Cucumber 136

Sweet Summertime Smoothie 137

Banana Green Smoothie 138

Index **139**

Introduction

Green foods are very likely the most nutritionally precise foods to meet the needs of human beings. Let's look at the ways they are the perfect food to nourish every cell, prevent risk, and keep us lean and energetic.

Protein

Let's begin with protein, since people in the Western world are rather preoccupied with this topic. Certainly protein (along with carbohydrates and fats) is needed in our diet and is, indeed, very important to build muscle mass and maintain the health of tissues throughout the body.

People are consistently shocked to learn that, for instance, broccoli and spinach are more than 40 percent protein. But protein content is only one of the ways that greens are easily the most perfect, nourishing, disease-preventing foods anywhere on Planet Earth.

If you're looking to increase protein in your plant foods for a specific health reason, consider that spinach is highest, at 42 percent protein, and use it liberally in your healthy smoothies (while also getting a variety of greens). Try to make your smoothies as low in fruit as possible for your own taste.

You can certainly add protein powder, though most whey-and soy-based protein powders are fractionated, heat-treated, and not good for you. Many studies in the past decade show that soy is not the health food we thought it was for many years. Soy in its whole and fermented forms, used in moderation, are likely entirely appropriate. The problem is that we're being bombarded with far too much soy in the form of processed isolates (parts of the grain separated from the whole food). Soy lecithin, soy proteins, and many other derivatives are in thousands of grocery store offerings. Please avoid soy protein powders.

Chlorophyll and blood-building properties

One of the reasons greens are powerhouse foods is the plant energy derived from chlorophyll, which is the plant equivalent of hemoglobin in the human red blood cell. Chlorophyll neutralizes internal body odors and bad breath, and it mops up free radicals that cause cancer and all degenerative disease.

Calcium

Everyone knows that calcium (combined with vitamin D obtained by spending a moderate amount of time in the sun) builds strong bones. Many people think that dairy products are their best sources of calcium. In fact, while dairy is high in calcium, it's not particularly bioavailable to human beings. The foods highest in calcium highly useable by people are, of course, greens. Highest are collards, parsley, watercress, dandelion greens, beet greens, kale, and watercress.

9

Greens are a powerhouse of enzymes, vitamins, and minerals. They are, ounce for ounce, the most nutritionally dense foods on the planet because they're the lowest in calories and highest in micronutrients. Scientists have recently discovered a number of nutritional classes of micronutrient compounds, but we still don't know how they all work together to protect against cancer and disease. What we do know is that greens, unlike synthetic vitamins, contain those compounds that synergistically reduce our risk of myriad health problems.

Most leafy greens are extremely high in antioxidant vitamins A, C, and E that bind with and neutralize free radicals. They're a source of folic acid that helps prevent birth defects in babies, as well as magnesium, which is an easy nutrient to become deficient in. Their dark colors show that they're high in phytochemicals, including over 500 carotenoid antioxidants, flavonoids, and indoles working synergistically to give the eater of greens abundant health. No supplement can provide the perfect balance of nutrition that raw green food contains naturally.

Fiber

Millions of Americans depend on chemical derivative fiber supplements to compensate for their low-fiber diet. (Chemical drinks like Metamucil are not the same as natural plant fiber and can irritate and overstimulate your body's digestive system.) This is a tragedy with epic consequences, not least of which is skyrocketing colon cancer deaths. The colon will be healthy if we provide it, all day long, with lots of insoluble plant fiber. That bulk drags the length of our gastrointestinal tract, much like a broom, keeping its tissues clean and pink and healthy.

Fiber famously prevents all types of cancers and digestive problems, but it also reduces cholesterol and heart disease, and controls blood sugar by slowing sugar uptake in the bloodstream. It prevents gallstones, decreases diabetes risk, binds excess estrogen, and assists in weight loss by creating a sense of fullness and less desire to overeat.

You don't find many foods higher in fiber than greens. The insoluble fiber functions like a sponge in the gut, and can expand, soak up, and remove several times its own weight in toxic materials. Its importance cannot be overstated because it's the only way we have to move dead cells and many other wastes through the body in minimal time, avoiding the decomposing and diseased cells that result when food sits, undigested, in various parts of our digestive and elimination systems.

A quart or more of healthy smoothie daily is a phenomenal way to dramatically increase fiber in the diet.

A quart should provide 12-15 grams of fiber to your diet. The average American gets only 11 grams of fiber daily, so if you're coming from the standard American diet, your fiber will at least double by adding this single habit. The USRDA is 30 grams, though government standards are rather unambitious, politically motivated, lowest-common-denominator standards. You actually need 50-70 grams. Don't be daunted by those figures. Make a gradual increase but, above all, don't stay at the typical American's 10-15 grams per day, where your disease risk is very high.

The Benefits of Healthy Smoothies

Smoothies, big deal, you say. You've had them before. But, in the past, you've thought of them as a frozen-fruit treat. The whole point with healthy smoothies is to maximize the greens, to add foods to your concoctions that you know are good for you but you perhaps rarely eat. If you need to, start with more fruit and less greens, but work your way up to the maximum green content. Remember, that's the point.

The benefits are so enormous:

- You're going to eat amazingly nutritious green food you haven't been eating, maybe ever. When was the last time you ate a big plate of plain collards, chard, carrot tops, and celery? Have you ever? Especially plain without gobs of ranch dressing? Mustard greens, arugula, turnip greens, dandelion greens, beet greens, and chard don't end up in too many salads, even for the most health conscious among us. Even most rawfoodists are deficient in greens. Just the time to chew the above-described plate of greens would take 30 minutes—and add chopping time to that. But those items and more will be in your healthy smoothies every day.

- You don't have to use high-fat, chemical-laden salad dressings to "get it down." Another benefit of a smoothie versus a salad is that all healthy smoothie ingredients are whole plant foods, with low calories and little or no added fat. Any fat you do add will be from high-quality, plant-based sources. Many people are not aware that salad dressings you purchase in the store are full of toxic chemicals like the deadly excitotoxin monosodium glutamate or MSG (which goes by many names you may not recognize on a label); the very worst refined sweetener, high-fructose corn syrup; refined salt; and rancid, refined oils like soybean and other vegetable oils. Many salads end up being rather high in calories and having some of the same ingredients in junk foods. Infamously, McDonald's salads sometimes are as high in calories as their other meals.

- Healthy smoothie prep is the highest-impact task you can undertake in your kitchen: the highest and best use of your time. Healthy smoothie preparation is the biggest "bang for the buck" and the biggest "return on investment" of your time spent in food preparation.

- Salads involve chopping. Healthy smoothies made in a blending machine don't. Raw-food recipes involve peeling, cutting, arranging, and, often, many steps. Healthy smoothies involve throwing everything in the fridge in a blender and pouring it out into a jar. It just couldn't be simpler. You don't have to be a gourmet, and even people who don't cook at all can do it easily.

- You get more live enzymes in blended green drinks than in any other food. Drinking a quart a day of healthy smoothie addresses what the number-one deficit in the American diet is: lack of enzymes. Enzymes

13

are catalysts in all bodily functions, including digestion. Digestive enzymes break down food for storage, and while your body's organs can produce the needed digestive enzymes, those organs typically become exhausted in anyone eating a typical Western diet of dead, processed foods. You have, at best, according to most estimates, about 30 years' worth of enzyme-production capacity. Eating raw foods, particularly leafy greens that have intact enzymes, gives you energy that does not deplete your limited enzymatic capacity. (And I'm not including iceberg lettuce in the category of "leafy greens," because it's a low-nutrition food relative to other lettuces and is not easily digested by humans, so I suggest spending your food dollars on other greens for your smoothies.)

- Smoothies retain all the fiber in the plant, without massive cleanup, compared to juicing. Many of us "health nuts" have a Champion, Jack LaLanne, or Omega juicer collecting dust in a back cupboard and making us feel guilty. We've juiced in fits and starts. Healthy smoothies are packed with insoluble plant fiber. Insoluble plant fiber is the best broom: It cleans out the 100-plus feet of your entire digestive tract. Think of your greens as a little muscle-bound green guy: He can carry out of your body several times more than his own body weight in toxic compounds that arrived through food, air, water, and stress. No spoonful of chemically reduced Metamucil can do what the natural fiber in plants can do. (In fact, Metamucil can be a colon irritant.)

14

- After the number-one deficit described above, live enzymes, perfectly addressed by healthy smoothies, the number-two deficit in the Western diet is lack of overall plant fiber in the diet Because fiber is removed from refined foods, Americans eat an average of only 11-14 grams per day (you get that much or more in your healthy smoothie alone), and the USRDA recommendation is 25-30 grams. I strongly recommend that at least 40-50 grams is ideal. A chimpanzee in the wild (left to his own devices to choose his diet) eats 300 grams per day! Fiber lowers blood cholesterol level and stabilizes blood sugar. It prevents hemorrhoids and constipation and every disease of the colon. Eating plenty of plant fiber is the best and, really, only way to avoid colon cancer, a leading cause of death and misery in the U.S. Insoluble plant fiber, while not digested, is critical in removing toxins, including metals, from the body. It's found abundantly in greens, as well as vegetables, beans, whole grains, legumes, nuts, and seeds.

- Healthy smoothies are fast to prepare and fast to eat. I love that healthy smoothies are "fast food" that is healthful, since those two conditions don't coincide in the same food very often. I do love salads for sit-down meals, to further augment consumption of greens and vegetables. But, unlike a salad, I can make a healthy smoothie the night before and put it in a quart jar in the fridge.

- You have a lower impact on the environment and you're eating lower on the food chain. We first undertake a habit like this because of the personal gain, but what a fantastic side benefit that we benefit the environment as well. When you eat plant food, you're requiring one-twentieth the resources of the earth, in terms of acreage and water, as you do when you eat the same quantity of food in the form of beef. Further, all the scraps can go into a compost pile to become fertilizer for even more plant food later If you don't garden, you can still toss your scraps on the ground outside. Even if they go to the landfill, they decompose quickly, unlike boxes and plastic used for packaged foods that may never decompose. Consider that every bit of healthy smoothie you consume is that much of some other food you didn't eat. Your carbon footprint is smaller with every healthy smoothie you drink. And no animals have to die or be miserably penned up in a too-small stall or cage to satisfy your caloric needs today.

- Healthy smoothies actually taste good—almost anyone will drink them, including the vegetable-phobic and the very young!

Let's Get Started!

So, you say, I'm sold! How much should I drink, then?

You may want to work your way up from a lesser amount, but a great goal is to have a quart a day. A quart is 15 servings of greens and fruit based on the U.S. Recommended Daily Allowances serving sizes! For most people, that's 750-1,500 percent more vegetables and fruits than they're currently getting.

You won't "overdose" on healthy smoothies unless you have some very rare conditions where excessive vitamin K or another nutrient must be avoided. Sometimes you can "detox" by eating nothing but blended drinks for a day or even a few days. One woman chronicled months of how she lost over 100 pounds consuming nothing at all except healthy smoothies over five months in an online blog.

You may, if you haven't been on a highly plant-based diet for a while, experience diarrhea or other cleansing reactions. Those reactions are temporary, a manifestation of your body recognizing good building and cleansing materials coming in, and an opportunity to throw out diseased, toxic, waste materials.

Sometimes when our tired, clogged, overworked organs begin receiving excellent nutrition, they can become overwhelmed, and uncomfortable reactions result. Those reactions rarely last longer than two weeks and are usually, in fact, much shorter in duration. They commonly include headaches, digestive disturbances, skin breakouts or rashes, a feeling of sluggishness, sleep problems, or other symptoms. Be patient with your body and don't let a little discomfort allow you to quit the path.

What Tools Do I Need?

Only two blenders on the market are worth your money: Vita-Mix and Blendtec. They're not really blenders—they're really called whole-food machines because they're so competent and have so many uses that a regular blender cannot compete with. All other blenders burn up, and not only will you be frustrated by having to buy blender after blender when they do, but you'll also have to leave out hard-core ingredients, like big frozen strawberries and the stems of greens. You save money in the long run and have better blended drinks if you invest in the right machine the first time.

Other items I recommend you have on hand are quart jars and plastic lids (which can be obtained at any discount retailer like Walmart or Target), and a bottle washer to clean them out. Wide-mouth jars are easier to clean than regular jars.

How Do I Drink a Healthy Smoothie?

Digestion begins in the mouth. So "chew" your smoothie. The one downfall to blended foods is the tendency we have to "slam" them.

Don't lie awake in bed at night worrying that you didn't "chew" your healthy smoothie enough. You've done a very good thing to drink a healthy smoothie, any way that happens, even if it's fed straight from a tube into your stomach. (Still beats a Big Mac and fries, or pretty much anything you were eating before!)

But the best way to drink your healthy smoothie is, in fact, to "eat" it rather than drink it. That is, even though it's liquid, take the time to "chew" it to stimulate your salivary glands. Slower is better to increase the saliva that begins the digestion enzymatically before your food is in the fundus, or pre-stomach.

Buying & Storing Tips

Buying greens

Look for several things when you buy greens and fruit:

1.   Do they look colorful and fresh? Avoid wilted produce or yellow or dry leaves.

2.   Are they organic? They may cost more, but often at my own health food store, the organic bunches are larger than the conventional bunches at the regular grocery store, which is an important consideration. Know how much more you're willing to pay for organic items—25 percent more? 50 percent more? Base your decisions accordingly, but organic is worth more because nutrition is higher, according to many studies.

Some greens are sponges for pesticides like DDT and other carcinogens, making organic purchases that much more important and worth your dollars. These high-accumulation greens include mustard greens, collard greens, and spinach.

3.   Locally grown produce almost always tastes even better than the organic produce you can buy in the stores. That's because it's very fresh when you get it, not gassed and trucked across the country. Besides the fossil-fuel savings, you support local businesses and keep farmers from going out of business.

In addition to buying locally grown fruits and vegetables, I would also encourage you to ask your grocery store to stock local and organic produce. If enough people create the demand, the supply will follow.

Storing greens

Greens can be kept fresh for up to one week in the refrigerator, depending on how fresh they were when purchased. Twist off plastic bags that contain greens tightly or use a twist tie to keep out air and water and preserve their life.

Some ways to extend the life of your greens include the following:

1.   Wash greens in advance of using them, and keep them in sealable Ziploc bags.

2.   Put them in quart or half gallon jars, fill with water, and keep in the fridge.

3.   When you realize that you won't be able to use all your greens before they go bad, chop them, put them in freezer bags, and freeze them. Try to use them within a few weeks to minimize nutrient loss.

Some nutrients are lost through freezing, but it's still the best way to preserve foods. Dehydrating below 116 degrees is the second-best way to preserve nutrients.

After greens are blended, they begin to oxidize (cells begin to degenerate or "rust"). Ideally, we'd blend our drinks and consume them immediately. However, I'd encourage you to not feel guilty about keeping healthy smoothies in the refrigerator for up to 48 hours. If we're such purists that we insist on perfectly fresh smoothies, the end result for anyone living in the real world is that we just won't make healthy smoothies every day. And that would be the greater loss.

Sometimes practicality trumps the ideal situation. But screw a lid on your jar of smoothie tightly to minimize oxidation.

Selecting and storing fruit

Look for seasonal fruits in the summer that you enjoy in smoothies, and take them home by the lug or bushel. Wash, quarter, and pit them, put a handful for one smoothie recipe in a sandwich baggie, and freeze (or quick-freeze them on cookie sheets first so they don't clump together into a frozen mass). They can be used throughout the winter when preserved this way.

Fruit often should be kept on the counter, rather than in the fridge, to ripen more naturally using the gases from ambient air. Fruit better kept out of the fridge include bananas, apples, peaches, and nectarines. Keep melons and other fruits in the fridge.

Here are additional tips:

Apples: Keep them on the counter, not in the fridge, so they don't become "mealy." They give off ethylene gas that ripens other fruit, so don't put them with potatoes (they'll grow sprouts) or other fruit you don't want to become overripe quickly. (On the other hand, if you want to speed up the ripening of bananas, put them in a brown paper bag with an apple.)

Avocados: Keep them on the counter or windowsill until they ripen. They're ripe when they become black and have a little "give" when you squeeze them slightly. Green avocados ripen nicely but can take two to seven days to do so. When they do become ripe, put them in the fridge to slow the ripening; this extends the time you have to use them by up to a week. When you use avocados, add a bit of fresh lemon juice to slow the oxidation that turns the flesh brown.

Bananas: Keep them on the counter or on a banana hook, not in the fridge where they're unable to ripen naturally. They'll overripen too quickly if a lot of them are together, so keep them separate as much as possible. Bananas are perfect to eat when they begin to develop a small number of dark spots and the green is gone; this is when the starches in the fruit have converted into sugars. When they begin to develop too many black spots, if you won't be using the bananas in the next day or two, simply peel them, break them into thirds, freeze in Ziploc sandwich bags, and use later in smoothies. If they're stuck together, just whack the bag of frozen banana chunks on the counter and they'll break apart. Or you can individually quick-freeze them on a cookie sheet before putting them in baggies. If you peel a banana from the bottom up, the little strings peel off better.

If you want to accelerate bananas' ripening, put them in a paper bag with an apple and roll the top closed. The apple's gases speed that process up so you won't have green bananas the next day.

Melons: Keep on the counter if ripening is needed, or in the fridge if they're ripe and you want to extend their life. You can tell a cantaloupe is ready to eat when you smell the indented end of it and it has a fragrant, ripe smell. When the cantaloupe is green, you can't smell anything. (This does not work with thin-and smooth-skinned melons like honeydew. The best test for a honeydew or watermelon is to buy one with rough, brownish "bug bites" on the skin.)

Oranges and other citrus: Keep in the fridge.

Pineapples and mangoes: Keep on the counter if ripening is needed, or in the fridge if they're ripe and you want to extend their life. You can tell a pineapple is ripe if it has yellow undertones rather than green under the brown scales, and you can easily pull one of the leaves out of the top. A ripe mango will have some "give" to it when squeezed slightly, and a green one will ripen on the counter or windowsill in one to five days.

Tomatoes: Keep them on the counter rather than in the fridge to avoid them becoming "mealy," which is an unpleasant texture for most recipes.

How to Grow Your Own Greens

Planting a garden is the best way to make healthy smoothies inexpensive. It also enables you to have control over the quality of your food, as you can garden organically very easily. It has two other side benefits: self-reliance in an emergency and helping you teach your children good work and reward principles.

People who garden tend to eat much more fresh produce and have an advantage in any kind of emergency situation, such as job loss. It's an excellent habit to cultivate, to teach children the "law of the harvest" very directly, that what you sow (and make an effort at), you reap.

Many gardeners love to grow vegetables and then wonder what to do with it all when the plants offer up a yield. That's the beauty of your new healthy smoothie habit: a place to use all kinds of crazy green food, every day. And what you can't use, you can freeze.

Another advantage to growing your own food is your reduced dependence on fossil fuels. Our food supply has become very pricey in terms of fossil fuels utilized to put our food on boats, trucks, and airplanes. We have access to produce from all over the globe, but at what cost? When we buy local produce or, even better, grow our own, our carbon footprint becomes much smaller and we contribute to making the world a better place for those who will come after us.

Having your hands and feet in contact with the earth is energizing in a very elemental way. We were meant to have contact with the ground and, in fact, we pick up massive antioxidants from "grounding" — our feet being in contact with earth. We were meant to be in the sun, as well. Exposure to sun gives us much-needed vitamin D that must be obtained to work with calcium to build bone mass. Sunshine also gives us a sense of peaceful well-being and connection to life and nature.

What you'll need

You'll need a garden space (ideally with wood square-foot boxes) or pots for gardening on a patio if you have no backyard.

You may wish to buy compost to add to the soil, and consider building one or more compost boxes in your backyard to reuse plant waste. Composted materials should be partly green (your food scraps) and partly brown (dead leaves, for instance), and should be turned several times over the course of several months as they decompose. Any compost pile should take a few months to one year to break down into a rich fertilizer for use in your garden.

Consider purchasing a new or used full-sized freezer to put in the garage. After gardening, this is the second-best way to save money eating a plant-based diet. It can dramatically extend the life of your garden produce, giving you vegetables and fruits through the winter. It also allows you to buy seeds and nuts in bulk through co-ops.

What if I have no space?

Many communities offer gardening space for free or for a very small fee, so ask your city about its resources. You can also use pots on the smallest of patios or porches.

What should I grow?

Here are greens and fruits you can grow (and some root vegetables that have greens you can use), depending on the space you have. Some (like zucchini) aren't what you traditionally think of as greens, but you can certainly hide some in your smoothies.

Beets

Endive

Kale

Radishes

Strawberries (perennials)

Cabbage

Escarole

Lettuce (all varieties)

Raspberries

Swiss chard

Carrots

Goji berries

Mesclun (mixed greens)

Spinach

Zucchini

How do I grow greens?

Greens do best in a good loam or heavier soil, rather than light, sandy soils. They do well when manure is added to the soil in the fall and given time over the winter to become part of the soil. Chicken manure, which has the highest nitrogen levels, is the best because leafy greens use nitrogen heavily. Don't add "green" (or fresh) manure in the spring right before planting. If you do fertilize in the spring, make sure to use aged material that will not "burn" your fledgling plants.

Manure provides constant levels of nutrients for the plant, perfect for organic gardening. Giving your plants chemical fertilizers is the equivalent of you or me taking a synthetic vitamin: It's a shock of less-helpful nutrients, followed by starvation until the next fertilization.

Because you'll want a steady stream of greens for your smoothies over the course of many months, stagger your plantings. Usually if you have an invasion of pests, they'll focus on one patch and leave earlier plantings alone. This gives you time to deal with the pests before they overrun more of your garden.

Keep in mind that tender greens such as lettuce and arugula need to be harvested when they're young. Otherwise they get bitter. Staggered plantings are even more important if you want to extend your yield.

In general, greens need about an inch of water per week. Especially in the hottest part of the summer, spread that over two waterings per week. After the seed sprouts and you see a green shoot above ground, keeping the soil constantly moist is no longer necessary.

Pick your greens in the morning or evening, not in the heat of the day. They'll taste better and last longer in the fridge.

What about organic produce?

Besides cost savings and dramatically improved taste, home-grown vegetables have another huge advantage: They're easily grown organically. Some studies show that organic produce has higher concentrations of vitamins and minerals, and other studies have found that "conventional" (sprayed) produce is nutritionally equal to organic. The jury is out on whether nutrient levels are higher, but what is crystal clear is that non-sprayed produce is lower in toxic pesticide and herbicide residue. If you cannot afford organic produce (and even if you can), growing greens in your garden is an excellent option. If you do purchase conventional greens, using a quality vegetable wash (available at health food stores or online) and rinsing well will help reduce pesticide residues significantly. Remember that animal protein has higher concentrations of the same toxins because they build up in the organs and flesh, so don't make a decision to stay away from produce if conventional is the only kind you have access to. Alternative foods are worse.

Why should I consider square-foot gardening?

For limited spaces, or to make the most of the space you have, I highly recommend square-foot gardening, which maximizes the yield per foot of space. You're gardening based on squares instead of rows, which lets you get twice the amount of produce out of half the space.

In one square foot, you might have nine beets, or four lettuce heads, or one corn stalk or tomato plant. This method is eco-friendly because you use much less water than with traditional gardening. You also have less weeding and a space designed for better access, since the grow boxes are up off the ground. The author of the system says that square-foot gardening uses 80 percent less space, time (especially weeding), water, and money than the traditional method.

Sample Diet Plans

The three plans in this chapter are designed to help you get the most out of your healthy smoothies. Whether you want to quickly rid your body of toxins, lose weight in a safe and healthy way, or completely change the way you live, here you'll find the plan that will help you do it in a safe and healthy way.

Three-Day Green Fast (Detox)

For those transitioning from a fairly standard American diet, I recommend using this program only after a few weeks or even months of drinking a quart of healthy smoothie daily. The detoxification that can sometimes result from a green-smoothie cleanse, if your body is highly toxic, can be a shock to the body's systems. How do you know if you're highly toxic? Lots of chronic health conditions are just one sign. Another is a lifetime of drinking alcohol or smoking; a long period of time eating processed foods, soft drinks, and meat and dairy; and/or a habit of not drinking enough water.

So working your way up to a cleanse program like this, with slower cleansing by having a quart of healthy smoothie daily, is a good idea. You can skip this preliminary step if you've been eating lots of whole foods and raw vegetables and fruit for two months or more.

This three-day detox is easy, and great for:

- Losing several pounds quickly

- Giving the kidneys, liver, and digestive system a much-needed rest, reducing risk for kidney and gallstones or breaking up existing stones

- Recovering from a long trip or a period of poor eating

- Clearing impurities through your skin and achieving better skin health

You can undertake this detoxification program while living your normal life, with all its demands. You should be able to go to work, play your sports or work out like you normally do, and/or look after children. The beauty of it, rather than complete fasting, is that you'll have blood sugar support, good nutrition, and enough calories to maintain energy.

You may choose any of the recipes in this book to use in your three days. Stock up on the ingredients you'll need in advance. Make your full day of healthy smoothies early in the morning (about 96 ounces) so that they're prepared and waiting for you anytime you're hungry, making the temptation to eat other things less intense.

WHAT TO EAT:

- Eat nothing but healthy smoothies and, in between, drink 8-10 glasses of pure (preferably alkaline) water.

- Drink as much healthy smoothie as you want (any one of the recipes in this book that makes 3 quarts is a good one-day supply).

- Add 1-2 tablespoons of flax oil, or an avocado, to your pitcher of healthy smoothie daily.

- You may get hungry occasionally, but have some healthy smoothie whenever you want food.

Thirty-Day Fat Burner Cleanse (Weight loss)

This more significant program involves a commitment of a greater period of time, with greater gains, including:

- Losing ten pounds or more (for those needing to lose weight)

- Significantly strengthening organs of elimination

- Breaking up and eliminating much of the years' worth of hardened mucoid plaque in the 100-plus feet of the digestive tract

- Regaining colonic regularity with soft but formed stool

- Beginning to reverse some health conditions, especially with a transition to the "Healthy smoothie for Life" program when you're done

This program involves drinking half a gallon of healthy smoothies daily, plus eating other raw plant foods only. If you crave cooked food, steam some vegetables or bake a potato. Eat freely of these foods:

- Green salads and other raw salads

- Sprouted grains, legumes, nuts, and seeds

- Fruits (such as berries, bananas, citrus such as oranges and grapefruit, tropical fruits such as mangoes and pineapples, cherries, apples, pears)

- Vegetables of all kinds, such as yams or sweet potatoes, green beans, carrots, cauliflower, broccoli, asparagus, beets, turnips, celery, artichokes

- Fresh or dried herbs such as basil, mint, oregano, tarragon

- Up to cup seeds like flax, chia, sunflower, sesame, pumpkin, especially sprouted (soaked overnight)

- Up to cup nuts like raw almonds, cashews, filberts, macadamias (not salted/roasted varieties)

35

Optionally, you may eat:

- Small amounts of raw sauces and dressings, cold-pressed oils, or desserts made from raw ingredients

- Crackers made from seeds, nuts, and vegetables with a dehydrator

Avoid these foods:

- Coffee, tea, and alcohol

- White flour

- Refined sugars and chemical sweeteners (corn syrup, white sugar, NutraSweet, Splenda, etc.)

- Beef, poultry, fish, shellfish, pork

- Dairy products

- Oils except small amounts of virgin, cold-processed oils (like olive or coconut)

Healthy smoothie for Life (Permanent lifestyle change)

Drinking a quart of healthy smoothie daily achieves:

- Ideal weight for the long term

- Significantly reduced risk of disease

- Dramatic increase in energy

- A permanent change in digestive patterns, eliminating within 12-24 hours of eating

- Decreased desire for refined sugar

- Over the first year, elimination of heavy buildup of mucoid plaque in the digestive system as well as heavy metals and other toxic materials

- Reversal of mineral deficiency issues, so that nails strengthen and grow faster, hair thickens, and gray hair possibly returns to its natural color

- Increased sex drive and mitigated PMS symptoms or menstrual irregularity

Do this every day:

- Drink 1 quart or more of healthy smoothie daily (any time—breakfast, lunch, snack—in two or more sittings, whenever you want)

- Eat 60-80 percent raw plant food including greens, vegetables, fruits, nuts, seeds, and sprouted grains/legumes/nuts/seeds

- Eat the remainder of the diet with mostly whole grains and legumes, or steamed or lightly sautéed vegetables

- Eat less than 5 percent animal protein (preferably none except for yogurt or kefir daily)

- Eliminate or rarely eat sugar, white flour, animal flesh and dairy, refined salt, fast foods, and any other processed foods

What to Do about a Cleansing Reaction

Perhaps the most confusing thing about undertaking a committed healthy smoothie habit is when you're expecting good results and instead you feel pretty terrible. This is a common consequence, unfortunately, yet only a short-term one. When the body begins to recognize new, good materials coming in, all its systems grab the opportunity to begin using those materials to clean house and begin rebuilding. Many organs of elimination, including the colon, liver, kidneys, skin, and lymph system, go into high gear. They can sometimes be overwhelmed and clogged by a deluge of toxins trying to "get out" through various avenues.

Headaches

Diarrhea

Bloating

Cramps

Vertigo

Fainting

Runny nose

Skin breakouts

Nausea

Intestinal gas

Constipation

Dizziness

Lethargy or weakness

Mucus in the back of the throat

Liver pain

Depression

Mood swings

Emotional crisis

What should you do, then, if you experience any of these symptoms? For starters, recognize symptoms of discomfort as what they are: a good thing — and don't abandon a great new habit, though you may wish to slow down by decreasing your smoothie consumption for a few days.

39

Second, drink extra water to flush out built-up toxins that need help evacuating. That should be about eight glasses of water for the average person, perhaps more for people who have larger builds. Drink water 20 minutes or more before a meal, or two hours or more after a meal, so the water does not dilute gastric juices when food is in the stomach. Tips for getting enough water into your schedule include, first, getting in the habit of drinking a pint immediately upon waking up, because you wake up dehydrated. Second, drink a glass of water every time you pass a drinking fountain during your workday. (You don't have to drink it from the water fountain if you bring higher-quality water, but that can be your reminder.) Third, drink a glass or two when you're preparing dinner (since dinner prep usually takes 20 minutes or more). Finally, get in the habit of always taking a water bottle with you in the car, to and from work or the gym or running errands.

Some believe that the "cleansing reaction" is just a cop-out by those in "alternative health" fields when we don't know what a health problem is. However, if you begin to undertake good nutrition, or work with others who do, you cannot help but notice how common this phenomenon is.

How to Make Your Smoothies

Many people like to follow very specific instructions. However, part of the beauty of healthy smoothies is their free-form, creative, anything-goes nature. So, if you're already comfortable in the kitchen and a creative soul, just use the "template recipe" given here first. The beauty of this template recipe is it maximizes greens and minimizes fruit for the average palate. As you get off processed sugar, you may find you can tolerate and even enjoy higher proportions of greens, but most people who are open-minded about food like smoothies made with the proportions in the template recipe. For children previously raised on a processed-food diet, or for "picky eaters," you may want to start with more fruit and/or sweetener and fewer greens, and work your way to a better ratio.

Remember that the major point of the healthy smoothie, of course, is the greens. Putting a pinch of spinach into a fruit smoothie is better than nothing, but challenge yourself to get several servings of raw greens out of your blender adventures.

If you're easily bored and don't want a similar taste every day, then use the recipes.

I like to blend the water and greens first. I do this to ensure that the greens are completely pureed, as no one appreciates a chunk of greens in what is, by definition, supposed to be smooth. (We're less likely to be offended by a chunk of banana or strawberry!) The unfrozen fruits tend to be softer, so I add them after the green puree is done. They need less blending and I don't want to oxidize them more than is necessary. I also like maximum liquid in my blender to make the blending easier before adding frozen items like chunks of bananas or strawberries. Other people like to make their smoothies differently, and some blend fruit and water, and then greens. There's no "wrong" way to do it!

Remember that variety is not only the "spice of life" that makes eating fun, but it also provides a wide spectrum of nutrients. The more variety in greens and fruit (and other high-nutrition additions to your smoothies), the better! You may ask: "I don't like most greens, so is it okay if I just use spinach and my favorite fruits?"

The answer to that is yes, that's certainly better than nothing. However, I want to challenge you to try new things. You have available to you a huge variety of greens out there, many of which you may not be considering. You can find new ones you haven't tried before in Asian, Latin, or health food stores. Don't forget to try more of these:

Traditional Greens/Lettuces:

- Kale

- Red chard
- Butter lettuce
- Miner's lettuce
- Arugula
- Spinach
- Napa cabbage
- Tatsoi
- Parsley
- Rainbow Swiss chard
- Endive
- Romaine
- Mache
- Vegetable amaranth
- Red cabbage
- Bok choy
- Pac choi
- Radicchio
- Swiss chard
- Escarole
- Mixed greens (mesclun)
- Celery
- Collard greens
- Green cabbage
- Yu choy
- Mizuna

Tops of root vegetables, etc.:

- Beet greens
- Turnip greens
- Grape leaves
- Kohlrabi tops
- Carrot tops
- Dandelion greens
- Mustard greens
- Jerusalem artichoke tops
- Strawberry tops (organic)
- Radish greens
- Anise/Fennel greens

Sea Vegetables:

- Arame
- Nori
- Kelp
- Kombu
- Hijiki
- Wakame
- Dulse

Weeds:

- Purslane

- Lambsquarter
- Morning glory
- Japanese knotweed
- Creeping Charlie

Sprouts:

- Brocolli sprouts
- Fenugreek
- Quinoa
- Bean sprouts
- Radish
- Pea greens
- Alfalfa
- Clover

Herbs:

- Mint leaves
- Lemon grass
- Bay leaves
- Tarragon leaves
- Marjoram
- Cilantro (coriander)
- Basil leaves
- Horseradish root

- Chives
- Oregano leaves

Fruits for Healthy smoothies

I've never met a fruit yet that isn't great in smoothies! Use whatever is in season to save money. But my staples are bananas and frozen mixed berries. Bananas add a creamy texture. Frozen mixed berries make smoothies a darker color for people who revolt at the big green glass, as well as bring the sugar level down a bit and add lots of fiber. Pears are my third-favorite fruit ingredient because they're sweet and balance greens so perfectly. But you have many other options. These are ingredients you might consider, and this list is by no means comprehensive.

Apricots

Apples

Bananas

Blackberries

Blueberries

Boysenberries

Cherries, Bing

Cantaloupe

Cherries, pie

Cranberries

Crenshaw melon

Grapes

Guanabana

Grapefruit

Honeydew melon

Kiwi

Kumquats

Lemons

Limes

Marionberries

Mango

Nectarines

Oranges

Papaya

Pears

Peaches

Persimmons

Pineapple

Plums

Prunes

Raspberries

Star fruit

Strawberries

Tangerines

Tangelos

Watermelon

Superfood Additions for Smoothies

Use those exotic, high-impact nutrition items if you can afford them. If not, please don't worry about it—you're getting tons of fiber, vitamins, minerals, and enzymes from the simple greens and fruit combinations.

Smoothies don't have to contain expensive, exotic ingredients. But not all of the "other ingredients" discussed in this section are expensive.

Acai berries (pronounced "ah-sah-ee")

Acai is a very trendy health product showing up mostly in overpriced pasteurized juices sold through network marketing channels. It's native to the Amazon rainforest and, like gojis, it's off the chart in antioxidants and anthocyanins (also present in red wine), which have been studied for their heart-protecting benefits (but without the attendant health problems caused by alcohol). Like gojis, acai berries are also high in the essential fatty acids omega-6 and omega-9, and are very expensive.

If you want to spend the money, I would recommend buying the whole berries rather than concentrated juices. The juices are artificially high in sugars, even if they are natural sugars, and highly acidic as well. The nutrients may be concentrated, but pasteurized juices have no enzymes and, therefore, draw on the body's ability to manufacture them, and sugars are concentrated as well. Wherever possible, use the whole food rather than a processed version of them.

48

Aloe vera

Aloe vera is an inexpensive extra ingredient and something I would encourage everyone (except pregnant women, until further testing is done for that population) to use in healthy smoothies. You can buy these plants in nurseries, and they grow wild in some very warm climates, such as in Arizona.

Aloe vera has been extensively studied for its immune-stimulating effects, and hundreds of research papers have been published documenting some very interesting benefits. One I find most interesting is the fact that it contains vitamin B12, one of the only plant-based sources of this nutrient, so adding this ingredient to smoothies can help vegans and vegetarians achieve complete nutrition. Additionally, the plant has anti-inflammatory, antibacterial, and antifungal properties. It heals ulcers and reduces asthma symptoms.

Avocado

Avocado adds extremely nutritious fats to your smoothie; a small amount of fat aids the body in utilizing the minerals in greens. I highly recommend adding it to smoothies for babies and children, too, or anyone who might need to gain weight. (It's not a food that will promote weight gain, but because of its high monounsaturated fat content, it's higher in calories than most healthy smoothie ingredients.) Avocado is one of the most perfect first foods for a baby. It's extraordinarily high in lutein, a phytonutrient that promotes strong eyesight and retards degenerative conditions of the eye.

Other research shows that even short-term avocado consumption decreases total and LDL cholesterol.

Bee pollen

Bee pollen has been a fascination of European researchers for a long time. The dust from the stamen of blossoming plants collected from bees is fairly well documented to improve a lot of things most of us care about. First of all, it increases your energy throughout the day and stamina for physical activity — it's a powerhouse nutritionally, with 35 percent protein.

Studies suggest it has natural weight-loss properties that have been mimicked chemically in various weight-loss drug remedies. Bee pollen not only stimulates metabolism, but also suppresses appetite naturally. It slows aging and prevents cancerous tumors from developing.

It also contains a gonadotropic sex hormone and contributes to improved sexual performance and reduction of PMS symptoms. Perhaps, most interestingly, it may prevent seasonal allergies, like eating raw honey allegedly does, but in a more direct way and without the blood sugar impact.

Brewer's (nutritional) yeast
Brewer's or "nutritional" yeast is grown on barley, and it's often used as a supplement, especially by nursing mothers to increase milk supply. It's high in protein and is also extremely rich in B vitamins. It has been linked to the reduction of symptoms of diabetes, eczema, constipation, and hypoglycemia.

50

It's also one of very few plant sources of B12. Vegetarian lifestyles are often criticized for their low intake of vitamin B12, and while vegetarians may not actually be suffering from low B12 (depending on which study you look at), using aloe vera and nutritional yeast are good ways to address that if you're avoiding all red meat.

Cayenne pepper

Cayenne pepper has long been used not only for a "heat" spice, but also for the medicinal purpose of opening the arteries and preventing cardiac events. Dr. Christopher famously gave people a cup of "cayenne tea" (one teaspoon in hot water) after cardiac events and said they would always be up and around immediately because it works faster than any pill. Cayenne is well known to herbalists for its ability to accelerate and intensify the effects of other herbs. It'll add heat and interesting flavor to your smoothies, and also open your blood vessels, improving circulation; in addition, it's anti-nausea, anti-allergy, and anti-constipation. Research has shown that cayenne also has the ability to kill cancer cells on contact.

Chia seed

With so much focus on essential fatty acids (EFAs) and omega fats, the chia seed is a standout because it's 40 percent omega- 6 oil. So many people are taking EFA supplements that this whole food, with its high omega 6:3 ratio, is very attractive.

51

Chia seeds absorb ten times their weight in water, so they're good thickeners when soaked. They also give you a sense of fullness, a great aid in weight loss. Some think they absorb some food calories as well, making them a diet helper in more ways than one. They slow the conversion of carbohydrates into sugars and, therefore, help maintain stable blood sugar levels, great for everyone, especially diabetics.

You can sprinkle chia seeds on anything as they have a neutral flavor, and unlike flaxseed, they're digestible without needing to be ground. But, unlike flax, they're quite expensive.

Chocolate, raw

Organic chocolate bars and acai berries are often marketed together. (And no wonder — it's a delicious, if expensive, combination.)

Dark chocolate has been touted in recent years for its very high Oxygen Radical Absorbance Capacity (ORAC) score, which means high antioxidants and consequent ability to protect against free radicals that age us and cause disease. Some people are confused by this and think that chocolate products found in health food stores are, then, high-nutrition items. Most products, even those marketed to health nuts like you and me, have sweeteners added (sometimes even processed sweeteners) and are cooked to eliminate the benefits of enzymes. They also have additives like alkali that are not beneficial and can even be destructive. One network-marketed candy claims to be a health food, costs $60 per pound, is artificially sweetened, and isn't even organic. You can spend $10 a pound for raw dark chocolate bars in the health food stores, and that's still a pricey treat.

Coconut oil, liquid or meat

Raw coconut is prized for its antibacterial, antimicrobial, antifungal, and antiviral properties. Dr. Bruce Fife's The Coconut OH Miracle effectively covers the research on this rather miraculous food, showing how a fat is not always a fat. Non-Westernized Pacific Islanders have ideal height-weight ratios and virtually no heart disease; they're some of the most beautiful people on the planet. Their diet relies so heavily on coconut that, despite it being a "saturated" fat, the Pacific-Islander indigenous diet is sometimes as high as 60 percent calories from fat, with extremely low rates of overweight people. They don't suffer from anxiety and depression, and they don't get cancer.

Flax oil

If you don't know how to get flax oil in your diet, adding a few tablespoons to a blender container full of smoothie is easy. Minerals from greens are absorbed better when eaten with some fats, so putting flax oil in your healthy smoothie is a great idea. You'll never even notice it. A tablespoon daily is a good dosage for an adult to avoid inflammatory ailments; it also protects healthy cell membranes needed to keep toxic elements out but allow nutrients in. Flax oil has wide-ranging benefits uncovered in research in the past decade, involving the immune, circulatory, reproductive, cardiovascular, and nervous systems. It's rich in essential fatty acids, including the rare omega-6 and omega-9 nutrients that your body cannot manufacture itself and must receive from outside sources.

Ginger

Fresh ginger is not actually a root, but rather an underground stem. You peel the brown outer layer off and add an inch or two, or more, to any smoothie. It adds a lovely flavor, but it also has powerful anti-inflammatory, digestive-function strengthening, and anti-nausea properties. It's a great natural remedy for motion sickness, morning sickness, and intestinal gas. If someone struggles with feeling nauseous while starting a green-smoothie habit, I recommend adding as much ginger as you can. It's a warming herb that helps stimulate blood circulation and promotes decongestion, and it can help knock down a fever.

Goji berries

Goji berries are an interesting food because they've been consumed regularly by the Earth's longest-living people for at least the past 1,700 years, as well as used medicinally. The berries are 13 percent protein, unheard of for a fruit, and they will increase the protein ratio of almost any healthy smoothie.

They also have several B vitamins and vitamin E, also rare in fruits, 18 amino acids, and possibly more antioxidants than any other food ever studied (though dark chocolate is a competitor). Remember that antioxidants scavenge free radicals, literally mopping up those little cancer-causing destroyers in the body. Many of the compounds found in abundance in the goji berry are so newly researched that we're only just beginning to understand how these nutrients cause increased disease resistance.

Lemon peel

Lemon peel is another ingredient you can add almost daily.

Kelp and dulse

If you don't mind the seaweedy taste of sea vegetables like kelp and dulse, use these high-impact foods in your blender. Just a little bit is enough, and they're more thyroid nourishing than any other food. So if you're hypothyroid (as about 25 percent of women are in America, many of them undiagnosed), consider getting one or both of these foods in your daily diet. Healthy smoothies are an easy way to do that. Those who suffer with low energy and slow metabolism often have low thyroid problems. (And diagnosing it can be difficult, involving full-panel blood testing done by a hormone clinic, examining the interplay of several different variables.) Taking a thyroid hormone, especially synthetic drugs such as Synthroid and Cytomel, causes disease risk and can burn out the thyroid even more over time. Sea vegetables nourish and support the thyroid rather than jab and poke it (and thus wearing it out over time), like drugs do, to make it perform.

Maca root

Maca is a very trendy product from an ancient Peruvian food. It's a root related to turnips and radishes because it's been linked by research to endocrine health and a healthy libido. It's also said to improve energy levels throughout the day. So the aphrodisiac is used in South America to boost performance in a variety of areas. In powdered form, it's an easy addition to healthy smoothies.

Pomegranate juice

Pomegranate juice is another very hot product because of a few studies linking it to slowing growth of prostate cancer and arthritis, and reduction of breast and skin cancer. It's been linked to improvement of several cardiovascular measurements, including thinning the blood and improving blood flow, lowering LDS cholesterol, and increasing HDL ("good") cholesterol.

I'd prefer to see people use the whole fruit, which is available in the winter. You peel away the red outer peel and the inner white membranes to harvest the seeds, which look exactly like rubies. It's a little more labor intensive to take apart a pomegranate than to prepare other fruit. However, it's fun for children because the fruit is so beautiful and a bit of a treasure hunt.

All juices are concentrated, with high natural sugar content, and also quite acidic. The whole fruit (while lower in vitamin and mineral concentrations) achieves the same benefit of pomegranate juice without the downside of a product that lacks live enzymes and is high in sugar.

Sprouts

Sprouts are so easy to grow, yet most people don't eat them at all. They're living things, and they're little enzyme-packed powerhouses. When the seed, nut, or legume sprouts, all the enzyme potential is unlocked to go into that burst of energy that becomes a plant. You have the opportunity, at that unparalleled nutritional level, to steal that nutrition for yourself. Sprouts have the capacity to dramatically reduce your reliance on the body's need to manufacture enzymes and, consequently, steal from metabolic processes. When you eat them, you're oxygenating your body and starving cancer cells—think of eating sprouts as the very opposite of eating sugar and other toxic foods that nourish cancer and make your body a host for all kinds of immediate and future problems.

Wheat germ, raw

Raw wheat germ is extremely high in vitamin E and the B vitamins, so this is a great ingredient for women with PMS or menopausal symptoms. In addition, eating it prevents some birth defects, according to research. It'll help you achieve glossy hair, pretty skin, and strong nails. It adds a nutty flavor and thickness to the smoothie, so you'll want to add extra water when using this ingredient. It's a great way to add fiber to your diet, promoting colonic peristalsis and avoiding constipation and diseases such as colon cancer.

However, raw wheat germ goes rancid very quickly. Buy it in bulk at your health food store if you trust that the store has good product turnover and buys fresh product often. Taste it before using, and if it has an even slightly rancid taste, don't use it. Store it in the fridge for no more than a couple of months, preferably in an airtight container to slow oxidation.

Wheatgrass juice (fresh or powdered)

Wheatgrass was first famously studied and used extensively by Ann Wigmore, founder of Optimum Health Institute and a pioneer of many therapies still used now, 50 years later, in natural healing. She wrote The Wheatgrass Book, documenting its megapowerful healing properties.

Yogurt or kefir

Yogurt or kefir, particularly homemade, adds a creamy, smooth texture to smoothies. Even more importantly, they contribute to a healthy gastrointestinal tract by populating it with good micro-organisms that are your main defense against bacterial infections and other harmful micro-organisms. Most people have 10:1 bad microorganisms to good, and the ratio should be reversed for a healthy colon. The best way to address this is to eat yogurt or kefir daily and avoid foods (like dairy, meat, and processed foods) that feed the bad bacteria.

If you're going to purchase commercial yogurt or kefir, organic is better, and buy plain flavor rather than the excessively sugar-sweetened vanilla and other flavors. Goat yogurt is nutritionally superior to dairy (cow's milk) products. It's not mucus forming and is easier to digest, due to a smaller fat molecule that permeates semi-permeable human membranes without triggering the body's defense mechanism to flush out with mucus. People do not experience "lactose intolerance" with goat's milk products, and many who are lactose intolerant with regular milk do not experience those symptoms with dairy yogurt.

Sweeteners for Smoothies, and Sugar Restrictions

Stevia

If you're diabetic, hypoglycemic, or trying to cut down on sugar, using stevia as your smoothie sweetener (or use no sweetener at all) is wise. Stevia is 100 times sweeter than sugar, but it's derived from an herb and is natural (though processors do add fillers to the powdered versions and a base to the liquid versions), so you can use to tsp. to sweeten a full blender of smoothie. You can purchase stevia either powdered or in liquid drops at any health food store.

In Asia, stevia has been widely used and well known for decades, although it has not been studied in clinical trials.

Many forces, including governmental ones, conspired to keep stevia out of the hands of American consumers for many years, even banning it from the shelves of stores selling food. This was not because of any consumer complaints about side effects (no side effects of stevia have been documented as of this writing), but because of the monopolistic chokehold that the manufacturers of the artificial sweetener aspartame (NutraSweet) had on the American food industry.

Agave Nectar

My second-favorite smoothie-sweetening option nutritionally (and my favorite option taste-wise) is to use raw, organic agave nectar, derived from cactus plants. The big advantage of using agave rather than other sweeteners is that it has one-third the glycemic index of sugar and honey. It's a light syrup with a pleasant, neutral flavor that you won't notice, and it's sweeter than sugar. You can purchase it online or in health food stores, or inexpensively by the gallon or case.

Agave has gotten a bad rap lately, as allegations have been made that Mexican companies sometimes cut high-fructose corn syrup into agave. Madhava is a good brand, and they process their "raw" agave under 118 degrees. Some brands that advertise to be raw probably are not. So, if you can, use a brand that clearly states its commitment to cold processing, since that's how enzymes are preserved.

Dates

Dates are an ancient food very high in magnesium and calcium. As a whole, raw food, they're an excellent sweetener and will have less impact on blood sugar. Use an equivalent amount of dates to whatever is called for in the recipe for agave (a 1:1 ratio).

Honey

Honey is very concentrated and sweetens a healthy smoothie very well. The upside to this sweetener is, if used raw, it may have the ability to decrease or eliminate your seasonal allergies. Regarding raw honey, some theorize that the cross-pollination done by local bees provides a type of homeopathic remedy.

The downside to honey is that it's very high on the glycemic index, which means it provides a jolt to your blood sugar comparable to sugar and corn syrup. Honey is much higher in nutrients, of course, but for those with blood sugar issues, it's best avoided. When you use it, do so in small amounts.

Maple Syrup

Maple syrup is never technically raw, but its nutrient content is certainly much higher than sugar or corn syrup, and because of the pleasant flavor, many raw foodists favor it as a sweetener. It's also expensive. Grade B is more unprocessed and, therefore, better than Grade A. Use maple syrup in a pinch, but keep in mind that it's a concentrated sweetener that has a relatively high impact on your blood sugar, so agave and stevia are your best options.

Recipes

If you're new to healthy smoothies or are feeling a little wary of what your concoctions might taste like, start with this Template Recipe below.

Healthy Smoothie Template Recipe

Makes 8 cups of 100 percent raw smoothie.

64

Tips: For beginners and those trying to convert children, consider using less greens and more fruit (especially berries and bananas) in the beginning, gradually working up to a 50/50 ratio as described here. In this transition phase, use just the mild flavors like spinach, kale, collards, and chard. With kids, consider using only spinach the first few days, then sneak in chard, collards, and kale gradually. Add other savory or bitter greens only when your family is "expert" in healthy smoothies! Add a bit more water if you feel the smoothie is too thick.

- Put 2 1/2 cups filtered water in the blender.

Optionally, add:

- ½ tsp. stevia (herbal sweetener) or cup raw, organic agave nectar (low glycemic index)
- ¼ whole lemon, including peel (anti-skin cancer, high in flavonoids)
- 2-3 Tbsp. fresh, refrigerated flax oil (omega-3 rich oil)

Gradually add until, briefly pureed, the mixture comes up to the 5-cup line (or less if you're "converting"):

- ¾ to 1 lb. raw, washed greens, added up to 5 1/2 cup line:
- spinach, chard, kale, collards are your mainstays
- turnip, mustard, dandelion greens, arugula — use more sparingly, as they're spicy or bitter
- lettuces and beet greens are also good — use freely

- try avocado or cabbage or 1-2 stalks celery
- Puree the greens mixture for 90 seconds, until very smooth.

Gradually add fruit until the container is very full (8 cups or more), blend 90 seconds or until smooth:

- 1-2 bananas to add a creamy texture and sweetness
- 1-2 cups frozen mixed berries (tastes wonderful and makes the smoothie purple rather than green)

any other fruit to taste: our favorites are pears and peaches, but also apples, oranges, apricots, cantaloupes (with seeds—very high in antioxidants!), mangoes, pineapples, anything!

The more frozen fruit you add, the tastier your smoothie will be! You can save your smoothie in the fridge for up to two days—just shake well before drinking.

Little-or-No-Fruit Healthy Smoothie

Some of you want to skip the fruit in your smoothie altogether. Maybe you're trying to cut out sugars (even unrefined fruit sugar), or you're on the Candida diet, or you're diabetic or highly hypoglycemic. If so, try this all-healthy smoothie that is both highly edible as well as nutrition-packed and low in sugar. It also has some necessary and nutritious fat in the form of avocado.

This recipe is for die-hards only—the type who'll drink anything for health, regardless of taste. That said, it tastes better than you'd think!

- avocado
- large cucumber
- cups spinach
- large leaves collard greens
- leaves black kale
- 2-3   lemons, juice only (to taste)
- 1/2   cups water

optional: a few slices of Gala apples

Puree well and enjoy.

Important Notes before You Use the Following Recipes

The remaining recipes in this book have a yield of 6 pints, and are most easily made in a large (96-ounce) blender container. If you have the smaller, 64-ounce container that comes with your machine, you can still use these large-batch recipes, but you'll fill up your container before adding all the fruit. Just blend as much of the ingredient list that fits in the container until smooth, and pour half of the mixture out into your glass jars. Then add the rest of the fruit, blend again, and pour the remainder into the jars. Put a lid on the jars and shake well.

If you prefer smaller batches, just cut the recipes in half for a yield of approximately three pints.

Keep in mind that if three quarts are too much for you, you can save healthy smoothies for the next day. (That's as long as they'll last, though. By the third day, they'll have lost a lot of nutrition and will taste funky,

A single person can drink a quart that day, save a quart for the next day, and freeze a quart for a third day. This way, you're cutting your time and effort by two-thirds for the same benefit. It'll make a big difference in your ability to get excellent nutrition within your busy schedule. Instead of spending ten minutes in the kitchen daily, a single person can spend ten minutes every third day. Just remember to get the frozen smoothie out several hours before you want to use it, and shake it well before drinking.

I use spinach in most of these recipes. One reason is that it's not only high in protein, but also outstanding in virtually all nutritional measures. A more practical reason, though, is that it's easy to have spinach on hand. Using lots of spinach helps keep smoothie costs low. (Use other greens for taste as well as that all-important vitamin and mineral variety.)

Aloe and Apple

- $2^{3/4}$ cups water/ice
- 2   large spears of fresh aloe vera, cut from the plant (or cup bottled)
- 4   large collard leaves
- Spinach, added until mixture reaches 6-cup line
- 1-2   inches fresh ginger, peeled
- 2   large Granny Smith apples
- 2   bananas, frozen in chunks
- 3   cups frozen blueberries
- 1   tsp. stevia

Blend first 4 ingredients until smooth. Add fruit and stevia and blend until smooth. Serve immediately for best results, or refrigerate up to 24 hours in glass jars and shake well before serving.

Arugula Arame Attack

- 3 cups water/ice
- 2 large handfuls arugula
- ¼ cup arame or wakame, or 1 raw nori sheet (Asian sea vegetable)
- Spinach, added until mixture reaches 6-cup line
- 2 cups pineapple, preferably frozen in chunks
- 2 bananas, frozen in chunks
- 2 cups frozen blueberries, blackberries, or mixed berries
- 1 apple or pear tsp. stevia

Blend first 4 ingredients until smooth. Add fruit and stevia and blend until smooth. Serve immediately for best results, or refrigerate up to 24 hours in glass jars and shake well before serving.

Asian Healthy smoothie

You can experiment with a wide variety of Asian greens, sprouts, and cabbages in your smoothies by going to your local Asian market. Ingredients tend to be inexpensive in these small markets, as well.

- $2^{1/4}$ cups water/ice
- 8 cups loose bok choy and yu choy (coarsely chopped)
- 1 cup Chinese celery

- 1-2 cups bean sprouts 4 tangelos

- 2 bananas, frozen in chunks tsp. stevia

- 4 cups frozen mixed berries

Blend first 3 ingredients until smooth. Add remaining ingredients and puree until smooth and serve immediately (best, as sprouts oxidize and lose nutrition quickly when blended), or pour in glass jars and refrigerate for up to 24 hours.

Beet Blast

Beets are a good way to change the color of a smoothie radically for those averse to green. This recipe is a good starter for children who need a sweeter, milder smoothie to begin converting to smoothies as a way of life.

71

- $3^{1/4}$ cups water/ice
- 1 medium beet, washed well and quartered
- ¼ of a medium green cabbage, cut in chunks
- Spinach, added until mixture reaches 6-cup line
- 2 Tbsp. honey
- 2 apples (Cameo, Jonathan, Jonagold, or Gala)
- 2 bananas, frozen in chunks
- 2 cups pineapple, frozen in chunks
- 1/4 tsp. ground nutmeg

Blend first 4 ingredients for 60 seconds, then add remaining ingredients and blend until very smooth. Serve immediately, or refrigerate for up to 24 hours in glass jars and shake well before serving.

Big Black Cabbage Cocktail

- 3 cups water/ice
- 4 cups black cabbage
- Spinach, added until mixture reaches 6-cup line
- 1/4 cup raw, organic agave
- 2 pears
- 2 bananas
- 8 apricots, pits removed (or equivalent amount of frozen mixed fruit)

Blend first 3 ingredients until smooth. Add remaining ingredients and blend until smooth. Serve immediately, or refrigerate for up to 24 hours in glass jars and shake well before serving.

Black Kale Blackberry Brew

- $2^{3/4}$ cups water/ice
- 2 stalks celery
- 5 large leaves black (lacinato) kale
- ¼ whole lemon
- 2 Tbsp. flax oil
- 2-4 Tbsp. raw, organic agave
- Spinach, added until mixture reaches 6-cup line
- 2 cups chopped fresh pineapple (optionally frozen)
- 2 cups blackberries
- 2 bananas, frozen in chunks

Blend first 7 ingredients until smooth. Add fruit and blend until smooth. Serve immediately, or refrigerate for up to 24 hours in glass jars and shake well before serving.

73

Blended Salad

Many modern health complaints make eating a salad very difficult for those who suffer from them. If you like salad but can't tolerate the chewing, this recipe may be helpful for you. It makes one serving.

- 1 very large handful spinach
- 1 tomato
- 1/8 to 1/4 red onion
- ½ avocado or 1 Tbsp. extra virgin olive oil
- ¼ zucchini or yellow squash
- A few sprigs of cilantro (optional)
- 1 Tbsp. lemon juice
- Water to achieve desired consistency
- pinch of sea salt and freshly ground pepper to taste

Blend all ingredients until smooth, using minimal olive oil and water to achieve a consistency for blending. Eat with a spoon, or thin out with water to drink.

Broccoli Blitz

- $2^{3/4}$ cup water/ice
- ¼ cup raw, organic agave

- 2 cups of broccoli (florets and/or stems), or broccoli rabe (found in Italian or Asian markets)
- Spinach, added until mixture reaches 5-cup line
- 2 oranges, peeled and quartered
- 2 cups pineapple, chopped
- 2 bananas, frozen in chunks
- 2 cups frozen mixed berries

Blend first 4 ingredients until smooth. Add fruit and blend again until smooth. Serve immediately, or refrigerate for up to 24 hours in glass jars and shake well before serving.

Brussels Blaster

I have hated cooked Brussels sprouts since childhood. Here's a way to get their excellent, anti-cancer, cruciferous nutrition in your diet without cooking the enzymes out, and not even notice they're there.

- 3 cups water/ice
- 12 Brussels sprouts
- Spinach, added until mixture reaches 6-cup line
- 1 yellow grapefruit, peeled
- 3 cups frozen mixed berries
- 2 bananas, frozen in chunks
- 1 apple

75

- $^{1/2}$ cup raw, organic agave

Blend first 3 ingredients until smooth. Add remaining ingredients and blend until smooth. Serve immediately, or refrigerate for up to 24 hours in glass jars and shake well before serving.

Butterhead Brew

(Butterhead, Bibb, and Boston are different names for the same lettuce variety.)

- $2^{3/4}$ cups water/ice
- 1 head Butterhead, Bibb, or Boston lettuce, washed
- 1/2 cup clover/radish/alfalfa/fenugreek sprouts (any combination of those small seeds)
- Spinach, added until mixture reaches 6-cup line cup raw, organic agave
- 2 bananas, frozen in chunks
- 2 oranges
- 2 cups frozen blueberries
- 2 cups frozen fruit medley or other fruit

Soak ¼ cup of seeds overnight, strain, and allow to sit another 12-24 hours, draining several times a day. Blend the first 4 ingredients well. Add agave and fruit and blend again until smooth. Serve immediately (as sprouts oxidize quickly).

Cabbage Cool-Aid

- $2^{3/4}$ cups water/ice
- Green cabbage, added until mixture reaches 6-cup line (yu choy or bok choy works, too)
- 4 cups frozen mixed berries
- 2 bananas, frozen in chunks
- 2 large tart apples
- $1/4$ cup raw, organic agave

Blend first 2 ingredients until smooth. Add fruit and agave and blend until smooth. Serve immediately for best results, or refrigerate up to 24 hours in glass jars and shake well before serving.

Carrot Top Concoction

- $2^{3/4}$ cups water/ice
- Carrot greens from 6 carrots Spinach, added until mixture reaches 6-cup line
- $1/2$ tsp. stevia
- 2 tart-sweet apples (Jonathan, Gala, Cameo, etc.)
- 2 oranges
- 1 banana
- 1-2 cups frozen berries

Blend first 3 ingredients for 1-2 minutes, then add remaining ingredients and blend until smooth. Serve immediately, or refrigerate for up to 24 hours in glass jars and shake well before serving.

Chia Choice

- $3^{1/4}$ cups water/ice
- 1 Tbsp. chia seeds
- Red leaf lettuce and/or chard leaves (with stems), blended into mixture to 6-cup line
- $1/2$ tsp. stevia
- 4 black plums, pits cut out
- 2 bananas, frozen in chunks
- 3 cups frozen berries
- Optional: dash of hot sauce

Blend first 3 ingredients until smooth. Add all other ingredients and blend well. Serve immediately, or refrigerate in glass jars for up to 24 hours and shake well before serving.

Cranapple Yogurt Crave

(A good winter choice, as all these ingredients are available November to March.)

- $2^{1/2}$ cups water/ice
- 1 cup yogurt
- 2 leaves chard, including stems
- 2 leaves collards, including stems
- Spinach, added until mixture reaches 6.5
- $1/3$ cup raw, organic agave
- 2 cups cranberries
- 2 cups blueberries
- 1 banana, frozen in chunks
- 3 Cameo apples

Blend first 6 ingredients until smooth. Add remaining ingredients and blend again until smooth. Serve immediately, or refrigerate for up to 24 hours in glass jars and shake well before serving.

Dandelion Delight

4 cups dandelion greens, coarsely chopped (wild/unsprayed, or found in health food stores)

½ tsp. stevia

¼ cup frozen orange juice (freshly squeezed and frozen in ice cube trays — 2 large ice cubes is ¼ cup)

Spinach, added and blended to the 6-cup line

2 oranges

2 bananas, frozen in chunks

¼ whole lemon

Frozen berries added until container is very full

Blend first 4 ingredients until smooth. Add fruit and blend until smooth. Serve immediately, or refrigerate for up to 24 hours in glass jars and shake well before serving.

Dilly Summer Drink

- $2^{3/4}$ cups water and ice
- $1/3$ cup fresh dill weed
- 4 cups mesclun (mixed spring greens)
- Spinach, added until mixture reaches 6-cup line
- ½ tsp. stevia

- $1/8$ whole lemon

- 4 nectarines, pits removed

- 2 bananas

- 2 cups frozen mixed berries

Blend first 4 ingredients until smooth. Add remaining ingredients and blend until smooth. Serve immediately, or refrigerate for up to 24 hours and shake well before serving.

Endive Energy Express

- $2^{3/4}$ cups water/ice

- Spinach, added until mixture reaches 4-cup line

- Curly endive, added and blended up to 6-cup line

- $1/4$ cup raw, organic agave

- 3 cups frozen mixed berries

- 4 Clementines

- 2 bananas, frozen in chunks

Blend first 3 ingredients well. Add agave and fruit and blend until smooth. Serve immediately, or refrigerate for up to 24 hours in glass jars and shake well before serving.

Everything + The Kitchen Sink Garden Smoothie

- $2^{3/4}$ cups water/ice
- 4 cups radish, carrot, strawberry, and/or beet tops, washed very well
- 1 cup weeds like purslane, dandelion, morning glory, or lambsquarter
- Spinach, added until mixture reaches 6-cup line
- $1/2$ tsp. stevia
- 3 cups frozen mixed-fruit blend
- 2 bananas, frozen in chunks
- 2 cups frozen mixed berries

Blend first 4 ingredients until very smooth. Add stevia and fruit and blend until smooth, immediately, or refrigerate for up to 24 hours in glass jars and shake well before serving.

Glorious Green Leaf

- $2^{3/4}$ cups water/ice
- 1-2 heads green leaf lettuce (or added up to 6-cup line when blended)
- 1-2 inches fresh ginger, peeled
- $1/8$ to $1/4$ whole lemon
- $1/4$ cup raw, organic agave
- 2 cups pineapple, frozen in chunks

83

- 2 oranges, peeled

- 2 bananas, frozen in chunks

- 2 cups frozen mixed berries

Blend first 3 ingredients until smooth. Add fruit and agave and blend until smooth. Serve immediately for best results, or refrigerate up to 24 hours in glass jars and shake well before serving.

Gobs of Goji

This is an easy smoothie to make in the winter because all these ingredients are available in stores, even in cold climates.

Goji berries, native to the Himalayas and Tibet, are a secret of longevity for some of the world's longest-living peoples.

- $3^{1/2}$ cups water/ice

- 1 cup dried (or fresh) goji berries — if fresh, decrease water by ½ cup

- 3 large collard leaves, including stems

- 5 small kale sprigs, including stems

- Spinach, added until mixture reaches 6-cup line

- $1/3$ cup raw, organic agave

- 1 banana, frozen in chunks

- 1 cup frozen blackberries

- 12 large frozen strawberries

- 3 apples or oranges

Soak goji berries in the water for the smoothie 30-60 minutes in advance. Then add all greens and blend until smooth. Add agave and fruit and blend again until smooth. Serve immediately, or refrigerate for up to 24 hours in glass jars and shake well before serving.

Grapefruit Cilantro Booster

- $2^{3/4}$ cup water/ice
- 2 cups cilantro
- 10 dates, pitted
- Spinach, added until mixture reaches 6-cup line
- $1/2$ tsp. ground cinnamon
- 1 large pink grapefruit, peeled
- 1 D'Anjou pear
- 2 bananas, frozen in chunks
- $1/4$ whole lime, unpeeled
- 2 cups frozen mixed berries

Blend first 4 ingredients until smooth. Add remaining ingredients and blend until smooth. Serve immediately, or refrigerate for up to 24 hours in glass jars and shake well before serving. (This recipe becomes stronger tasting if not consumed immediately.)

Green Chocolate Cooler

Rave taste-test reviews from my four kids, and higher in calories and protein than most healthy smoothie recipes—good for those involved in athletic training. This is bright green but chocolate flavored!

- 3 cups ice water
- 1/2 vanilla bean
- 2 large kale leaves
- Red leaf lettuce, added until mixture reaches 6-cup line
- 1/4 cup cacao nibs or powdered chocolate
- 2 Granny Smith apples
- 2 mangoes, peeled and pits removed
- 2 bananas, frozen in chunks
- ½ cup almond butter
- ½ cup raw, organic agave

Blend first 4 ingredients until smooth. Add remaining ingredients and blend until smooth. Serve immediately, or refrigerate for up to 24 hours and shake well before serving.

Kale Tangelo Tonic

- $2^{1/2}$ cups water
- 1 bunch curly kale
- 10-ounce bag baby spinach
- 5 tangelos or Clementines
- 1 banana, frozen in chunks
- 3 cups frozen mixed berries
- ¼ whole lemon
- ¼ cup raw, organic agave

Blend first 3 ingredients well. Add remaining ingredients, puree until smooth, and serve immediately, or refrigerate for up to 24 hours in glass jars and shake well before serving.

Key Lime Broccosprout Blend

- $2^{3/4}$ cups water/ice
- 4 key limes (whole)
- 1 cup broccoli sprouts (from health food store or sprout them yourself)
- Spinach, added until mixture reaches 6-cup line
- 3 D'Anjou pears
- 2 bananas, frozen in chunks
- 2 cups frozen mixed berries

- 1 tsp. stevia

Blend first 4 ingredients until smooth. Add remaining ingredients and blend until smooth. Serve immediately, or refrigerate for up to 24 hours in glass jars and shake well before serving.

Kiwi Banana Krush

- $2^{3/4}$ cups water/ice
- 6 medium chard leaves
- Spinach, added until mixture reaches 6-cup line
- 6 kiwis, peeled
- 1 banana, frozen in chunks
- 2 pears
- 3 cups frozen berries (until blender container is very full)
- ½ tsp. stevia or 2 Tbsp. raw, organic agave

Blend first 3 ingredients until smooth. Add fruit and stevia/agave and blend until smooth. Serve immediately for best results, or refrigerate up to 24 hours in glass jars and shake well before serving.

The Kumquat Question

- $2^{3/4}$ cups water/ice
- 2 cups anise (fennel greens) (save the white fennel bulb for slicing into
- salads)
- Spinach, added until mixture reaches 6-cup line
- 1 cup kumquats (including skin)
- 3 bananas, frozen in chunks
- 3 cups frozen mixed berries
- $1/3$ cup raw, organic agave

Blend first 3 ingredients until smooth, then add remaining ingredients and blend again until smooth. Serve immediately, or refrigerate for up to 24 hours in glass jars and shake well before serving.

Late-Summer Apricot Watercress Divine

- $2^{3/4}$ cups water/ice
- 1 bunch watercress
- 3 leaves kale (any kind)
- Spring greens, added until mixture reaches 6-cup line
- $1/4$ lime
- 5-6 ripe apricots (optionally frozen in chunks)
- 2 ripe peaches (optionally frozen in chunks)

- 1 banana, frozen in chunks
- 1 cup blueberries

Blend first 5 ingredients until smooth, add fruit and blend again until smooth. Serve immediately, or refrigerate for up to 24 hours in glass jars and shake well before serving.

Latin Healthy smoothie

- 3 cups water
- 1/2 bunch cilantro
- 2 inches fresh ginger, peeled
- 1/2 tsp. cayenne pepper
- ¼ cup raw, organic agave
- Spinach and/or collards, added until mixture reaches 6-cup line
- 2 star fruit, coarsely chopped
- 1/2 lime, washed and quartered (including peel)
- 2 bananas, frozen in chunks
- 2 pears or apples
- 2 cups frozen mixed berries

Blend first 6 ingredients until smooth. Add remaining ingredients and blend until smooth. Serve immediately, or refrigerate for up to 24 hours in glass jars and shake well before serving.

90

Mango Meltaway

- $2^{3/4}$ cups water/ice
- 2 stalks celery, chopped in fourths
- Spinach, added until mixture reaches 6-cup line
- $^{1/2}$ cup cashews
- ½ tsp. vanilla
- ½ tsp. stevia
- 2 large mangoes, peeled and cut away from the pit
- 2 bananas, frozen in chunks
- 2 cups frozen blueberries
- ½ cup plain, nonfat yogurt or kefir

Blend first 4 ingredients until smooth, then add remaining ingredients and blend again until very smooth. Serve immediately for best results, or refrigerate up to 24 hours in glass jars and shake well before serving.

Melon-Seed Melange

It looks very green, but it's tasty! These ingredients are best when they're available in the very late summer or early fall.

- 1/4 cup raw, organic agave
- 2 cups water

- 2 cups green cabbage

- 1 cup chopped parsley

- Spinach, added until mixture reaches 6-cup line

- 4 cups cantaloupe, including all the seeds, etc., in the center (cut off peel)

- 2 bananas, frozen in chunks

- 12 medium to large frozen strawberries

Blend first 5 ingredients until very smooth. Add remaining ingredients and blend again until smooth. Serve immediately, or refrigerate for up to 24 hours in glass jars and shake well before serving.

Mixed Green Maca Madness

- 3 cups water/ice

- Mixed spring greens, added to mixture up to 4-cup line

- Spinach, added until mixture reaches 6-cup line

- ¼ cup maca root powder

- 1/2 tsp. lemon-flavored liquid stevia

- 2 cups pineapple

- 2 bananas, frozen in chunks

- 4 cups frozen berries

Blend first 3 ingredients until smooth. Add remaining ingredients and blend until smooth. Serve immediately for best results, or refrigerate up to 24 hours in glass jars and shake well before serving.

Mustard Greens Mambo

- $2^{3/4}$ cups water/ice
- 2 large leaves (and stems) mustard greens, coarsely chopped
- 4 cups romaine, coarsely chopped
- Spinach, added until mixture reaches 6-cup line
- $2/3$ tsp. powdered stevia
- 2 bananas, frozen in chunks
- 16 ounces frozen blackberries
- 1 small papaya, peeled (include the seeds in the smoothie)
- 2 apples, pears, or oranges

Blend first 4 ingredients until smooth, then add remaining ingredients and blend again until smooth. Serve immediately, or refrigerate for up to 24 hours in glass jars and shake well before serving.

One Really Grape Smoothie

- $2^{3/4}$ cups water/ice
- 4 large handfuls mixed salad greens (such as sold in a tub at Costco)

93

- Chard leaves (and stems), added until mixture reaches 6-cup line
- 1 banana, frozen in chunks
- 3 cups frozen mixed berries
- 2 cups seedless grapes (any kind)
- 2 Gala or Braeburn apples (add until blender container is very full)
- ¼ cup raw, organic agave

Blend first 3 ingredients until smooth. Add fruit and agave and blend until smooth. Serve immediately or refrigerate for up to 24 hours in glass jars and shake well before serving.

Pear Date Puree

- 2³/⁴ cups water/ice
- 4 cups rainbow chard
- Spinach, added until mixture reaches 6-cup line
- ¼ whole lemon
- 1 inch fresh ginger, peeled
- 6 large dates, or 1/4 cup chopped dates (rinsed)
- 3 large D'Anjou pears
- 3 cups Arozen mixed berries

If possible, soak dates in water for 30 minutes. Blend first 6 ingredients until smooth. Add pears and berries and blend again until smooth. Serve immediately for best results, or refrigerate up to 24 hours in glass jars and shake well before serving.

Pollen Persimmon Potpourri

Bee pollen is famous for its aphrodisiac qualities as well as its ability to enhance your energy and many other health benefits. Raw local honey may help eliminate or reduce seasonal allergies.

- $2^{3/4}$ cups water/ice
- 2 Tbsp. bee pollen
- 2 Tbsp. raw honey
- $1/2$ tsp. cinnamon
- ¼ tsp. nutmeg
- Spinach, added until mixture reaches 6-cup line
- 2 cups persimmons, chopped
- 1 banana, frozen in chunks
- 2 sweet apples, like Red or Golden Delicious
- 2 cups frozen blackberries

Blend first 6 ingredients until smooth. Add remaining ingredients and blend until smooth. Serve immediately, or refrigerate for up to 24 hours and shake well before serving.

95

Pomegranate Potion

Pomegranate juice has been an expensive "fad" health food for the past several years, as it's unusually high in polyhenols, tannins, and anthocyanins; the juice is higher in antioxidants than even green tea. Some studies documented decreases in blood pressure and cholesterol or those drinking the juice daily or a year. I'd still rather see you eat the whole food than a juice with a concentration of high sugars. You'll have lots of fiber from the pomegranate seeds, if not the concentration of nutrients that are not combinations found in nature anyway. Just buy a pomegranate when they're in season, peel away the red outer peel, break open the parts inside, and pop the ruby-like seeds out to eat. Children love the "treasure hunt" of removing the beautiful, juicy seeds in a pomegranate.

- $2^{3/4}$ cups water/ice
- 5 large curly kale leaves
- Spinach, added until mixture reaches 6-cup line
- ¼ cup raw, organic agave
- 4 tangerines or 2 oranges
- 1 banana, frozen in chunks
- Seeds of 1 large pomegranate (1 cup or more)
- 2-3 Granny Smith apples
- 2 cups mixed frozen berries

96

Blend first 3 ingredients until smooth, then add remaining ingredients and blend again until smooth. Serve immediately, or refrigerate for up to 24 hours in glass jars and shake well before serving.

Rad Raspberry Radicchio

- 3 cups water/ice
- 2 large handfuls radicchio or red/purple cabbage
- Spinach, added until mixture reaches 6-cup line
- ¼ cup raw, organic agave
- 2 cups frozen berries of any kind
- 3 tart-sweet (pink) apples, like Fuji or Jonathan
- 2 bananas, frozen in chunks

Blend first 3 ingredients until smooth. Add agave and fruit and blend until smooth. Serve immediately for best results, or refrigerate up to 24 hours in glass jars and shake well before serving.

Red Leaf Rocks

- 1 cup ice
- $1^{3/4}$ cups water
- 1 head red leaf lettuce, washed
- Collards, added until mixture reaches 6-cup line

97

- $^{1/2}$ lime (or 1-2 key limes), unpeeled

- 1 avocado, peeled and pit removed

- 2 Granny Smith (green) apples 1 banana, frozen in chunks

- 4 cups frozen mixed berries

- $^{1/2}$ tsp. stevia

Blend first 4 ingredients until smooth. Add fruit and stevia and blend until smooth. Serve immediately for best results, or refrigerate up to 24 hours in glass jars and shake well before serving.

Red Pepper Mint Julep

- $2^{3/4}$ cups water

- 1 red bell pepper

- 1 large stalk celery

- ¼ whole lemon (including peel)

- 1 handful fresh mint leaves

- Spinach, added until mixture reaches 6-cup line

- ½ tsp. stevia

- 1 Tbsp. bee pollen

- 2 apples

- 2 cups frozen mixed berries

- 4 cups frozen mixed fruit

- 1 banana, frozen in chunks

Blend first 6 ingredients until smooth. Add remaining ingredients and blend until smooth. Serve immediately, or refrigerate for up to 24 hours and shake well before serving.

Red Smoothie

- $2^{3/4}$ cups water/ice
- 4 cups beet greens, coarsely chopped
- Spinach, added until mixture reaches 6-cup line
- $^{1/2}$ tsp. stevia
- 2-ounce bag frozen pitted cherries
- 2 bananas, frozen in chunks
- 12 agricots, pitted

Blend first 3 ingredients until smooth. Add remaining ingredients and blend until smooth. Serve immediately or refrigerate for up to 24 hours in glass jars and shake well before serving.

Romaine Rounder

- $2^{3/4}$ cups water/ice
- 2 stalks celery
- 1 carrot

99

- Romaine lettuce, added until mixture reaches 6-cup line
- ½ tsp. stevia
- 1 ripe Bosc pear
- 8 apricots (preferably halved and frozen) or 4 peaches
- 2 bananas, frozen in chunks
- 2 cups frozen mixed berries

Blend first 4 ingredients until smooth. Add stevia and fruit and blend until smooth. Serve immediately for best results, or refrigerate up to 24 hours in glass jars and shake well before serving.

Savory Sweet-Hot Smoothie

- $2^{3/4}$ cups water/ice
- 4 radishes and tops, washed well
- 3 ounces pea greens
- Spinach, added until mixture reaches 6-cup line
- ¼ cup chopped dates
- $1/2$ tsp. cayenne pepper
- 2 cups pineapple, preferably frozen in chunks
- 3 cups frozen berries
- 3 bananas, frozen in chunks

Blend first 4 ingredients until smooth. Add remaining ingredients and blend until smooth. Serve immediately for best nutrition (sprouts oxidize quickly), or refrigerate up to 24 hours in glass jars and shake well before serving.

Smooth Sunflowers

- 2³/⁴ cups water/ice
- 2 ounces sprouted sunflower greens (grow your own or purchase at health food store)
- Spinach, added until mixture reaches 6-cup line
- ¼ whole lemon
- 1 large Gala or Jonathan apple
- 2 bananas, frozen in chunks
- 2 small pears
- 2 cups frozen berries (or more, to fill container completely)

Blend first 3 ingredients until smooth. Add remaining ingredients and blend until smooth. Serve immediately, or refrigerate for up to 24 hours in glass jars and shake well before serving.

Sodium Dandelion Blast

Don't get sodium, the natural element and critical tissuebinder, mixed up with soduimchloride, the table salt. The former is highly necessary in your while the latter should be avoided. Celery is an outstanding contributor of sodium and is high on the maximum-nutrients-for-the-calorie scale, since you expend more calories eating celery than you get from it!

- $2^{3/4}$ cups water

- 2 large stalks celery

- ¼ whole lemon

- 2 inches fresh ginger, peeled

- 4 cups dandelion greens spinach, added and blended up to 6-cup line

- 2 oranges

- 2 bananas, frozen in chunks

- Frozen berries added and blended until container is very full

Blend first 6 ingredients until smooth. Add fruit and blend until smooth. Serve immediately, or refrigerate for up to 24 hours in glass jars and shake well before serving.

South Pacific Healthy smoothie

- $2^{3/4}$ cups young Thai coconut liquid (or water)

- 4-6 large dates

- Your favorite greens, added until mixture reaches 6-cup line

- 3 cups chopped fresh pineapple

- 1 cup young Thai coconut flesh

- 2 cups guanabana fruit or pulp (if you can find it, imported — if not, use any other fruit, like dark berries, if you don't want your smoothie to be bright green)

- 3 bananas, frozen in chunks

Blend first 3 ingredients until smooth. Add remaining ingredients and blend again until smooth. Serve immediately for best nutrition, or store for up to 24 hours in glass jars in the fridge, shaking well before serving.

Southern Turnip-Collard Watermelon Cooler

These are popular ingredients in the South but can be found elsewhere, as well, in the summer.

- 1 cup water
- 4 cups watermelon chunks
- 4 turnip green leaves (and stems), coarsely chopped
- 4 large collard leaves (and stems), coarsely chopped
- ¼ cup raw, organic agave
- 2 pears (or apples, oranges, etc.)
- 12 ounces frozen rasberries
- 2 bananas

Blend all ingredients together until very smooth. Serve immediately, or refrigerate for up to 24 hours in glass jars and shake well before serving.

Sweet Beet Slam

- 3 cups water/ice
- 1 large English cucumber (no need to peel it)
- 1 large carrot
- Beet greens, added until mixture reaches 6-cup line
- ½ tsp. cinnamon
- 1/3 cup agave
- 2 large, ripe pears (added till container is very full)
- 3 cups frozen mixed berries
- 1 banana, frozen in chunks

Blend first 4 ingredients until smooth. Add remaining ingredients and blend until smooth, immediately, or refrigerate for up to 24 hours in glass jars and shake well before serving.

Tomato Tonic

- 2 cups water/ice
- 1 large English cucumber, washed and chopped into 2-inch
- 1 stalk celery, quartered
- 1 large carrot, quartered
- 3 large, ripe Roma tomatoes
- 1 large handful spinach

- 2 cloves fresh garlic
- Pinch sea salt
- Freshly ground pepper to taste
- Tabasco or hot sauce to taste

Blend all ingredients until very smooth. Serve immediately.

Watercress Avocado Dream

- $2^{3/4}$ cups water/ice
- 1 inch fresh ginger, peeled
- ¼ cup raw, organic agave
- 1 bunch watercress
- 2 stalks celery
- 1 ripe avocado
- Spinach, added until mixture reaches 6-cup line
- 2 pears
- 2 bananas, frozen in chunks
- Frozen mixed berries, added until container is very full

Blend first 7 ingredients in the order and quantities given. When mixture is very smooth, serve immediately, or refrigerate for up to 24 hours in glass jars and shake well before serving.

Peach-Mango Green Smoothie

Here is a super delicious meal-replacement green smoothie that will fill you up. It is a great blend of year-round tropical fruits and seasonal, summer fruit; such as peaches. This is a creamy smoothie with a distinctive peach flavor accented with mango.

- 4 peaches, pitted
- 2 banana, peeled and sliced
- 1 large mango, pitted and peeled
- 4 cups spinach
- 8 ounces water

Add all the ingredients except the spinach in your blender. Hit the pulse button a few times. Add the spinach and blend on high until the smoothie is creamy. Pour into a glass and serve.

"Post Workout" Smoothie

This is a mild Green Smoothie recipe with the best of both worlds in protein and simple sugars, giving your body everything it needs after a great workout. Green smoothies are great raw food meals that are easy to make and take on the run.

106

- 2 cups spinach

- 1/2 romaine head

- 2 stalks celery

- 3 bananas, peeled and sliced

- 3 oranges, peeled and quartered

- 1 cup blackberries

Place all ingredients in blender and blend until thoroughly combined. Pour into a glass and serve.

Glow Inside and Out Ultimate Green Smoothie

You will not only look healthy, but you will also feel healthy with this Green Smoothie. It takes only a few minutes of your day to prepare this amazing treat.

- 1 1/2 cup water

- 1 romaine lettuce head, chopped

- 4 stalks celery

- 2 apples, cored and chopped

- 1 banana, peeled and sliced

- 1/3 cup organic cilantro

- 1/3 cup parsley

- 1/2 cup lemon juice

Add the water and chopped head of romaine to the blender. Start the blender on a low speed, mix until smooth. Gradually moving to a higher speed, add the herbs, celery and apples. Add the banana and lemon juice last. Mix until thoroughly combined. Pour into a glass and serve.

Easy Kid-Friendly Green Smoothie

Kids love green smoothies! If the green color "scares" them just come up with cool, fun names like the "Incredible Hulk Smoothie." Just get creative, kids love them!

- 1 frozen banana, peeled and sliced
- 1/2 cup frozen pineapple, peeled and sliced
- 3/4 cup water
- 1 cup spinach
- 1 tablespoon raw honey (children under 1 year of age should not consumer honey)

Place all ingredients in blender and blend until thoroughly combined. Pour into a glass and serve.

Green Java

Looking for a morning coffee alternative? This is something that will wake you up and give you a boost of energy? Wheat grass is pure pick-me-up; pure energy, and with all the vitamin C from the oranges, it is everything you need to get up and get going.

- 1 bunch of wheat grass
- 2 oranges, peeled and quartered
- 1 banana, peeled and sliced
- 1 cup water
- 1 of cup ice

Place all ingredients in blender and blend until thoroughly combined. Pour into a glass and serve.

Chocolate Green Smoothie

If the green factor wigs you out, trust me, you can't taste the spinach. Raw chocolate (cacao) is a healthy smoothie addition, and it sure cures chocolate cravings!

- 1 frozen banana
- 1/2 cup frozen berries
- 1 tablespoon raw cacao

109

- 1/2 cup frozen pineapple, peeled and sliced
- 1 cup water
- 1 tablespoon raw honey
- 2-3 tablespoons hemp seeds
- 1 tablespoon coconut oil

Place all ingredients in blender and blend until thoroughly combined. Pour into a glass and serve.

Green Jungle Monkey Smoothie

You will definitely go bananas with this delicious smoothie.

- 4 bananas, peeled and sliced
- 1/2 cup strawberries
- 1 cup spinach
- 2 cups water

Place all ingredients in blender and blend until thoroughly combined. Pour into a glass and serve.

Cheerful Cherry Green Smoothie

Looking to sneak in an extra serving of leafy greens into your day to support youthful skin and a healthy glow? Toss a handful of spinach into this cherry and banana smoothie - your taste buds will never know the difference. Your body, however, will love the benefits.

- 1 cup cherries, pitted and frozen
- 1 banana, peeled and frozen
- 1 cup spinach
- 1 cup water
- 4 ice cubes

Place all ingredients in blender and blend until thoroughly combined. Pour into a glass and serve.

Tropical Pineapple

Bring the tropics and good health to you with this tropical treat.

- 1/2 fresh pineapple, peeled and sliced
- 2 bananas, peeled and sliced
- 1 orange, peeled and sliced
- 1/2 head romaine lettuce
- 2 cups water

111

Place all ingredients in blender and blend until thoroughly combined. Pour into a glass and serve.

Kale and Banana Smoothie

This Kale and Banana smoothie is perfect for the summer. You will feel refreshed, healthy, and full of energy.

- 2 bananas, peeled and sliced
- 2 tablespoons hemp seed
- 1 cup frozen blue berries
- 2 1/2 cups water
- 5 kale leaves

Place all ingredients in blender and blend until thoroughly combined. Pour into a glass and serve.

Berry Smoothie with Bee Pollen

Bee pollen has been used for centuries as it is widely believed to increase energy, libido, and strengthen the immune system! Have allergies? Bee pollen is known as a natural way to reduce bothersome allergies.

- 1 cup water
- 1 cup purple or red grapes
- 1/2 cup blueberries (fresh or frozen)
- 2 bananas

112

- 1 handful of red kale
- Half-teaspoon bee pollen (start with a few granules if taking for the very first time)

Place all ingredients in blender and blend until thoroughly combined. Pour into a glass and serve.

Kale and Pear Smoothie

Drink for strong healthy bones, healthy heart and an improved immune system—you get it all in this delicious green smoothie! Kale may not be the first thing you think of when it comes to making a great smoothie—but it is definitely one of the best!

- 1 cup green grapes
- 1 orange, peeled
- 1/2 pear, peeled and sliced
- 1 frozen banana, peeled and sliced
- 1 cup kale
- 1 cup water
- 2 cups ice cubes

Place all ingredients in blender and blend until thoroughly combined. Pour into a glass and serve.

113

Banana-Orange Green Smoothie

This delicious smoothie is low fat, low sodium, low cholesterol, heart healthy, gluten-free, vegetarian, vegan, and raw! You can be enjoying your drink while having the peace of mind that it is healthy.

- 2 bananas, peeled and sliced
- 3 oranges, peeled and quartered 1 romaine lettuce head
- 4 cups water

Place all ingredients in blender and blend until thoroughly combined. Pour into a glass and serve.

Green Protein Smoothie

This green protein smoothie is the best of both worlds! Packed with protein, loaded with nutrients and antioxidants as well as a healthy boost of protein! And, to make things even better, it tastes delicious!

- 1 banana, peeled and chopped
- 1 cup spinach, packed
- 1 scoop protein powder
- 1/3 cup pomegranate juice
- 1 cup filtered water
- 1/2 cup ice cubes
- 1 tablespoon ground flax seeds

Place all ingredients in blender and blend until thoroughly combined. Pour into a glass and serve.

Healthy Green Coconut Smoothie

- 2 frozen bananas, peeled and sliced
- 2 handfuls spinach
- 1 cup almond milk
- 1/4 teaspoon cinnamon
- 1 teaspoon vanilla
- 1 tablespoon coconut oil

Place all ingredients in blender and blend until thoroughly combined. Pour into a glass and serve.

Ginger-Carrot with Pineapple Smoothie

Ginger and pineapple blend together for a spicy and warming smoothie recipe for a chilly winter day. This mix of ingredients makes it very rich in vitamins and minerals that will help your body keep its wellbeing.

- 1 cup pineapple, peeled and cubed

115

- 1 cup carrot, grated
- 1 banana, peeled and sliced
- 1/2 inch fresh ginger, grated
- 6 ounces almond milk

Place all ingredients in blender and blend until thoroughly combined. Pour into a glass and serve.

Apple-Pineapple Tropical Fusion Green Smoothie

Apples and pineapples taste great together in this tropical fusion smoothie. They make the perfect blend to try out a new type of leafy green - escarole. Escarole is a type of endive. It has broad leaves and is much less bitter other endives or even kale.

- 8 ounces almond milk
- 2 apples, cored
- 2 cups pineapple, cubed
- 1 stalk celery
- 1 escarole lettuce head

Add all the ingredients except the greens in your blender. Hit the pulse button a few times. Add the greens and blend on high until the smoothie is creamy. Pour into a glass and serve.

Tropical Pineapple-Papaya Green Smoothie

When the snow is falling, along with the temperature dropping, this drink will put you in a tropical sunshine mood. This smoothie if very sweet and so it is perfect for blending with celery and parsley.

- 1 cup papaya, cubed
- 1 cup pineapple, cubed
- 1 medium banana, peeled and sliced
- 2 stalks celery, chopped
- 1 cup parsley
- 4 ounces almond milk

Place all ingredients in blender and blend until thoroughly combined. Pour into a glass and serve.

Meal Replacement Green Smoothie

Here's a tasty green smoothie for you. Sweet coconut is the dominant flavor that mingles with a hint of tropical fruitiness. Mango and papaya make great accents in this smoothie. It can be a satisfying meal replacement, and it will keep you energized for hours when you are on the go.

- 1 young Thai coconut, water and flesh
- 1/2 large mango, peeled and pitted

117

- 1/4 large papaya, peeled and pitted
- 1 tablespoon flax seed
- 1 tablespoon maca powder
- 1 scoop rice protein
- 1 head of green leaf lettuce

Add all the ingredients except the lettuce in your blender. Hit the pulse button a few times. Add the lettuce and blend on high until the smoothie is creamy. Pour into a glass and serve.

Cherry-Citrus with Dandelion Greens Smoothie

Dandelions provide an excellent source of calcium, iron, beta-carotene, vitamin K and other nutrients. While dandelion greens are quite bitter compared to spinach, the flavor can be masked effectively with citrus, and sweetened with bananas.

- 2 cups dandelion greens, chopped
- 1/2 cup cherries, pitted and frozen
- 1 orange, peeled and deseeded
- 2 small bananas, peeled
- 1 scoop rice protein powder 6 ounces water

Add all the ingredients except the greens in your blender. Hit the pulse button a few times. Add the greens and blend on high until the smoothie is creamy. Pour into a glass and serve.

Raw Food Breakfast Smoothie

Who said that raw can't be healthy? This smoothie is high in vitamin A, low in sodium and cholesterol You can enjoy this invigorating drink daily.

- 1 frozen banana, peeled and sliced
- 1 scoop Chia Seeds
- 1 handful raw cashews
- 1 handful raw sunflower seeds
- 1 tablespoon raw organic coconut oil
- 3 ice cubes
- 1 kale leaf, chopped
- 1/4 cup almond milk

Place all ingredients in blender and blend until thoroughly combined. Pour into a glass and serve.

"The Newbie" Smoothie

This smoothie lets you experiment. You can try out what flavor and consistency you like. Just adjust to your preference.

- 3 bananas, peeled and sliced
- 2 apples, cored and deseeded
- 1 cup mixed berries, frozen
- 3 slices pineapple, peeled and sliced
- 1/2 cup water
- 1 bunch mixed greens

Place all ingredients in blender and blend until thoroughly combined. Pour into a glass and serve.

Organic Green Smoothie

Organic ingredients make a healthier you. These ingredients prevent the occurrence of stroke and heart attacks. Eat healthy to live healthy.

- 1/2 inch fresh ginger, peeled
- 1/4 lemon
- 2 apples, cored
- 5 kale leaves (stems removed)
- 1 avocado flesh

- 1 cup water

Place all ingredients in blender and blend until thoroughly combined. Pour into a glass and serve.

Alcohol Detox Smoothie

This alcohol detox smoothie recipe is vital for the healthy regeneration of your liver. Using a solid combination of cleansing foods to detoxify the body from alcohol, this smoothie can be used to recover after a night of over-indulgence or to support a longer-term alcohol detox program.

- 2 cups of mixed berries, frozen
- 1 coconut, water and flesh
- 2 bananas, peeled and sliced
- 2 tablespoons of milk thistle seeds
- 1 cup water

Grind milk thistle seeds in a coffee grinder or good blender. Cut open the top of the coconut and place the milk and coconut flesh in your blender. Add ground seeds, bananas and berries to the blender. Blend for 30 seconds or until thoroughly liquidized. Add water until your smoothie reaches the consistency you prefer. Pour into a glass and serve.

Strawberry-Raspberry Heart Healthy Smoothie

Berries in a smoothie are always a good choice. Berries are loaded with antioxidants. This smoothie has a mix of sweetness and sourness to it. Everyone will surely enjoy this healthy drink.

- 6 ounces almond milk
- 1 cup spinach leaves
- l cup strawberries
- 1 banana, peeled and sliced
- 1/2 vanilla bean
- 1/2 cup raspberries
- 1/2 teaspoon raw maca powder

Place all ingredients in blender and blend until thoroughly combined. Pour into a glass and serve.

Green Drink

If you are not used to healthy green drinks, you may find them a bit "earthy" in the beginning. I bet one day you will be craving green drinks just like this recipe.

- 2 apples, cored
- 2 cups spinach

122

- 1 medium cucumber

- 3 sticks celery, chopped

- 1/2 ginger root, peeled

- 1 bunch parsley

- 1 lime, juiced

- 1/2 lemon, juiced

Place all ingredients in blender and blend until thoroughly combined. Pour into a glass and serve.

Heart Healthy Smoothie

This drink will give you a healthy heart. This drink will give your heart the energy to pump the blood that your body needs.

- 1 banana, peeled and sliced

- 1 orange, peeled and quartered

- 1 cup mixed berries

- 1/4 avocado, pitted

- 3 cups baby spinach

- 1 tablespoon ground flax seed

- 4 ounces filtered water

Add all the ingredients except the greens in your blender. Hit the pulse button a few times. Add the greens and blend on high until the smoothie is creamy. Pour into a glass and serve.

The Healthy Green

This drink is purely green; it is sweet, sour, bitter and a little spicy.

- 1 bunch watercress
- 1 green apple
- 1 lime
- 1/4 cucumber
- 4 mint leaves
- 1 banana, peeled and sliced
- 1/4 cup water
- 1 cup ice

Place all ingredients in blender and blend until thoroughly combined. Pour into a glass and serve.

Groovy Green Smoothie

Get groovy after drinking this smoothie! It is healthy, yet tasty. Everyone will surely love this drink.

- 1 banana cut in chunks
- 1 cup grapes
- 1 small tub vanilla yogurt
- 1/2 apple, cored and chopped
- 1 1/2 cups fresh spinach leaves

Place all ingredients in blender and blend until thoroughly combined. Pour into a glass and serve.

Cashew Peach Green Smoothie

Cashews are a great way to get your protein as an alternative to meat, fish and eggs. Peaches, on the other hand, are loaded with fiber.

- 1/3 cup cashews, unroasted and unsalted
- 2 tablespoons raw honey
- 1/4 cup peaches, frozen
- 1 1/3 cup water
- 1 cup fresh spinach
- 4 ice cubes

Soak cashews for 15-20 minutes in your blender to maximize the creaminess of the cashews. Place all ingredients in blender and blend until thoroughly combined. Pour into a glass and serve.

Blueberry Green Smoothie with Almond Butter

A nutritious smoothie for breakfast is a wonderful and delicious way to dial up your body's overnight detoxification and slimming work.

- 1 cup blueberries, frozen
- 1 cup spinach
- 1 tablespoon almond butter
- 1/2 banana, peeled and sliced
- 1 cup water
- 4 ice cubes

Place all ingredients in blender and blend until thoroughly combined. Pour into a glass and serve.

Green Smoothie with Peanut Butter

Dark leafy green vegetables and juices are great for reversing signs of aging, and to help you achieve a healthy glow.

- 1 banana, peeled and sliced
- 2 tablespoons peanut butter
- 1 cup of spinach
- 1 cup water
- 4 ice cubes

Place all ingredients in blender and blend until thoroughly combined. Pour into a glass and serve.

Blueberry Green Smoothie

Green Smoothies are an easy and a delicious way to incorporate more leafy greens into your day. By eating more leafy green vegetables you give your body the nutrients it needs to help keep your energy high and your skin looking youthful

- 1 cup blueberries, frozen
- 1 cup of spinach
- 1/2 banana, peeled and sliced
- 1 cup water
- 4 ice cubes

Place all ingredients in blender and blend until thoroughly combined. Pour into a glass and serve.

127

Banana Mango Green Smoothie

Green smoothies give you a chance to sneak a few more nutritious leafy green foods into your day that you wouldn't necessarily eat otherwise. Leafy green foods are loaded with vitamins and minerals, antioxidants and blood alkalinizers for superior health and energy.

- 1 1/2 cups mango, peeled and sliced
- 1/2 frozen banana, peeled and sliced
- 1 1/2 cups coconut water
- 1 sprig fresh basil
- 1 cup mixed greens

Place all ingredients in blender and blend until thoroughly combined. Pour into a glass and serve.

Summer Blueberry Green Smoothie

This smoothie is the perfect way to combat the summer heat. Grab this smoothie and go to the beach. Enjoy this drink under the sun.

- 1/2 cup almond milk
- 1 frozen banana, peeled and sliced
- 1 cup baby spinach
- 1 cup blueberries

128

- 1/2 cup ice cubes
- 1 tablespoon honey

Place all ingredients in blender and blend until thoroughly combined. Pour into a glass and serve.

Mango Banana Green Smoothie

The mix of the banana and the mango plus the greens is the perfect combination. The addition of the cashew adds protein to this delicious smoothie.

- 1 cup cashews
- 1/2 cup water
- 1 tablespoon raw honey
- 1 banana, peeled and sliced
- 1 mango, peeled and sliced
- 1/2 romaine lettuce heart

Throw cashews into blender with water and raw honey. Blend until creamy. Add banana and mango. Blend until smooth. Add romaine lettuce. Blend. If the consistency is like a milk shake, you are done. If not, add a bit more water. You do not want this smoothie to be too thick or thin. Pour into a glass and serve.

High Protein Green Smoothie

A Green Smoothie for breakfast is one of the easiest ways to get started with your diet changes. A Green Smoothie for breakfast helps elongate your body's powerful overnight rejuvenation and slimming work.

- 1 cup water
- 1 cup strawberries, frozen
- 1 scoop protein powder
- 1/2 banana, frozen
- 3 small collard green leaves, stems trimmed

Place all ingredients in blender and blend until thoroughly combined. Pour into a glass and serve.

Cleansing Green Smoothie with Parsley

Parsley is eaten in the spring to help your body naturally let go of weight. Using parsley year-round helps fire up your body's natural digestion and crud removing work.

- 1 pear, sliced in half and cored
- 1 handful of flat-leafed parsley, stems trimmed
- 1 tablespoon honey
- 1/4 avocado, peeled and pitted

130

- 3/4 cup water
- 5 ice cubes

Place all ingredients in blender and blend until thoroughly combined. Pour into a glass and serve.

Kickin' Kale Strawberry Smoothie

Kale is king packed with fiber and vitamins, but it can also be a little intimidating to eat. However, kale can be tamed quite nicely in a smoothie. Combine a few leaves of curly green kale with a few sweet strawberries and a small banana to make a great smoothie.

- 1 cup of curly green kale, stems removed
- 1 cup strawberries, frozen
- 1 frozen banana, peeled and sliced
- 1 cup water
- 1 cup ice
- 1 tablespoon raw honey

Place all ingredients in blender and blend until thoroughly combined. Pour into a glass and serve.

Kale Smoothie with Pear

Kale has a strong flavor, but if you combine it in just the right way, it can be a great variation on a traditional green smoothie. This healthy combination can liven up your day.

- 1 cup curly green kale stems removed
- 1 pear, frozen and deseeded
- 1/2 frozen banana, peeled and sliced
- 1 cup water
- 1 cup ice

Place all ingredients in blender and blend until thoroughly combined. Pour into a glass and serve.

Kale Smoothie with Papaya

Looking for a new smoothie recipe to mix up your week? This Kale Smoothie with Papaya may be just the thing. The subtle addition of the basil will surely be a hit.

- 1 1/2 cup curly green kale
- 1 frozen banana, peeled and sliced
- 1/2 cup papaya, frozen
- 3 tablespoons fresh basil leaves

- 1 cup water
- 1/2 cup ice

Place all ingredients in blender and blend until thoroughly combined. Pour into a glass and serve.

Green Lightening

This drink is easy to make. No matter how busy you are, you can spare a few minutes of your time to make this drink.

- 3/4 kale, chopped
- 1 inch ginger, peeled
- 1/2 lemon
- 1 cup apple juice
- 1 cup ice cubes

Place all ingredients in blender and blend until thoroughly combined. Pour into a glass and serve.

Mango Green

A simple yet healthy smoothie featuring Romaine lettuce which has high levels of vitamin C, K, and A is a great source of folic acid.

- 3 large mangos, peeled and sliced
- 1 banana, peeled and sliced
- 1/2 head romaine lettuce
- 1 cup water

Place all ingredients in blender and blend until thoroughly combined. Pour into a glass and serve.

Berry Blast

If you like berries, then you will love this berry smoothie, delicious and refreshing.

- 1/2 pint raspberries
- 1/2 pint blueberries
- 2 bananas, peeled and sliced
- 3 big handfuls of baby spinach
- 2 cups water

Place all ingredients in blender and blend until thoroughly combined. Pour into a glass and serve.

Velvety Green Smoothie

Rich in antioxidants, minerals, vitamins and fiber, this smoothie can help reduce the aging of body cells and help to reduce blood sugar levels.

- 1 handful dandelion greens
- 1 banana
- 1 handful parsley
- 3 large mangos, peeled and sliced
- 2 cups water

Place all ingredients in blender and blend until thoroughly combined. Pour into a glass and serve.

Delightful Strawberry

For all you strawberry lovers out there!

- 1 pint strawberries
- 1 apple, cored and sliced
- 1 banana, peeled and sliced

135

- 2 cups spinach
- 2 cups water

Place all ingredients in blender and blend until thoroughly combined. Pour into a glass and serve.

Zesty Banana

A quick, easy, and delicious smoothie to start your day.

- 1 bananas, peeled and sliced
- 2 oranges, peeled and sliced
- 1 head romaine lettuce
- 4 cups water

Place all ingredients in blender and blend until thoroughly combined. Pour into a glass and serve.

Cool Mint Cucumber

Stay "cool as a cucumber" with this refreshing smoothie. The cucumbers will make your skin glow!

136

- 4 cucumbers, peeled and sliced
- 2 pears
- 1 bunch fresh mint leaves
- 2 cups water

Place all ingredients in blender and blend until thoroughly combined. Pour into a glass and serve.

Sweet Summertime Smoothie

A delightful summertime treat.

- 1 banana, peeled and sliced
- 4 cups watermelon
- 6 romaine leaves
- 1/2 lemon

Place all ingredients in blender and blend until thoroughly combined. Pour into a glass and serve.

Banana Green Smoothie

Leafy greens, including baby spinach, romaine lettuce, kale, water cress, Swiss chard and even basil, help to keep your skin looking fresh and youthful. Embrace more greens in your day with this Banana Green Smoothie.

- 1 banana, peeled and frozen
- 1 cup of organic spinach
- 1 cup coconut water
- 4 ice cubes

Place all ingredients in blender and blend until thoroughly combined. Pour into a glass and serve.

Index

A

almond, 86, 115, 116, 117, 119, 122, 126, 128
aloe, 51, 69
apple, 23, 24, 70, 75, 101, 124, 125, 133, 135
apples, 23, 35, 66, 67, 69, 72, 77, 78, 80, 85, 86, 90,
    93, 94, 95, 96, 97, 98, 103, 107, 108, 116, 120, 122
apricots, 66, 72, 89, 100
avocado, 34, 50, 66, 67, 74, 98, 105, 120, 123, 130

B

banana, 24, 42, 78, 80, 84, 87, 88, 90, 94, 95, 96, 98,
    104, 106, 107, 108, 109, 111, 113, 114, 116, 117,
    119, 122, 123, 124, 125, 126, 127, 128, 129, 130,
    131, 132, 134, 135, 137, 138
bananas, 23, 24, 35, 42, 46, 65, 66, 69, 70, 71, 72, 73,
    75, 76, 77, 79, 81, 82, 83, 84, 85, 86, 87, 89, 90, 91,
    92, 93, 97, 99, 100, 101, 102, 103, 105, 107, 110,
    111, 112, 114, 115, 118, 120, 121, 134, 136
bean sprouts, 71
beet, 9, 12, 65, 72, 83, 99
bell pepper, 98
berries, 28, 35, 46, 48, 52, 55, 65, 78, 79, 81, 84, 85,
    88, 92, 95, 96, 97, 100, 101, 102, 109, 112, 121,
    134
blackberries, 70, 73, 84, 93, 95, 107
blueberries, 69, 70, 76, 80, 90, 91, 112, 126, 127, 128,
    134
bok choy, 70, 77

C

cabbage, 43, 66, 72, 77, 92, 97
cantaloupe, 24, 92
carrot, 12, 83, 99, 104, 116
Carrot, 44, 78, 115
cashews, 35, 91, 119, 125, 126, 129
cayenne pepper, 90, 100
celery, 12, 35, 66, 70, 73, 91, 98, 99, 101, 102, 104,
    105, 107, 108, 116, 117, 123
chocolate, 52, 53, 55, 86, 109
cilantro, 74, 85, 90, 107
coconut, 36, 53, 102, 110, 115, 117, 119, 121, 128, 138
collard, 20, 67, 69, 84, 103, 130
cranberries, 80

cucumber, 67, 104, 123, 124, 136

D

dates, 62, 85, 94, 95, 100, 102

F

flax oil, 34, 54, 65, 73

G

garlic, 105
ginger, 54, 69, 83, 90, 94, 102, 105, 116, 120, 123, 133
grapefruit, 35, 75, 85
grapes, 94, 112, 113, 125

H

honey, 50, 61, 62, 72, 95, 108, 110, 125, 129, 130, 131

K

kale, 9, 65, 67, 73, 84, 86, 87, 89, 96, 112, 113, 116,
    119, 120, 131, 132, 133, 138

L

lemon, 23, 65, 73, 74, 81, 82, 83, 87, 92, 94, 98, 101,
    102, 108, 120, 123, 133, 137
lemons, 67
lettuce, 14, 30, 31, 43, 76, 79, 83, 86, 97, 100, 107,
    111, 114, 116, 118, 129, 134, 136, 138

M

mangoes, 25, 35, 66, 86, 91
mangos, 134, 135
mixed berries, 46, 66, 70, 71, 75, 77, 82, 83, 84, 85, 87,
    89, 90, 94, 98, 100, 104, 105, 120, 121, 123
mixed-fruit, 83

N

nectarines, 23, 82

139

O

onion, 74
orange, 81, 111, 113, 118, 123
oranges, 35, 66, 75, 76, 78, 81, 84, 85, 93, 96, 102,
103, 107, 109, 114, 136
organic agave, 61, 65, 72, 73, 74, 76, 77, 80, 82, 83, 84,
86, 87, 88, 89, 90, 91, 94, 96, 97, 103, 105

P

papaya, 93, 117, 118, 132
peaches, 23, 66, 89, 100, 106, 125
peanut butter, 127
pears, 35, 66, 72, 87, 88, 90, 93, 94, 95, 101, 103, 104,
105, 137
pineapple, 25, 70, 72, 73, 75, 83, 92, 100, 102, 108,
110, 111, 115, 116, 117, 120
pomegranate, 57, 96, 114

R

raspberries, 122, 134
romaine, 93, 107, 108, 111, 114, 129, 134, 136, 137,
138

S

spinach, 8, 20, 41, 42, 65, 67, 69, 74, 87, 102, 104, 106,
107, 108, 109, 110, 111, 114, 115, 118, 122, 123,
125, 126, 127, 128, 134, 136, 138
Spinach, 29, 43, 69, 70, 72, 73, 75, 76, 78, 80, 81, 82,
83, 84, 85, 87, 88, 89, 90, 91, 92, 93, 94, 95, 96, 97,
98, 99, 100, 101, 105
squash, 74
strawberries, 18, 42, 84, 92, 110, 122, 130, 131, 135

T

tangerines, 96
tomato, 31, 74
turnip, 12, 65, 103

W

watercress, 9, 89, 105, 124

Y

yogurt, 38, 59, 60, 80, 91, 125

Z

zucchini, 28, 74

Made in the USA
Lexington, KY
13 October 2013